The Voice *Ra*

The Voice Ra,
formerly T.T.Rangarajan and founder of
Alma Mater, has transformed tens of
thousands of people by providing significant
breakthroughs in their lives. Be it top notch
businessmen, global leaders, musicians,
sportsmen or students, many have been able
to unleash their internal spirit that drives
them to excellence. Realising the great
hunger in the world for a new way of life,
The Voice Ra has now divined the new path,
Infinitheism.

infinitheism

For anyone who ardently desires abundance in any sphere of human endeavour - spiritual, emotional and material, Infinitheism is the path that provides breakthroughs and allows the human spirit to realise its humongous, boundless potential.

www.infinitheism.com

● ● ●

Ratria

The symbol of Infinitheism - Ratria, symbolises continuity, perpetuity and never ending evolution of the body, mind & soul.

Carry me with you in life,
and I will carry you through life.

To.

SAGARJI

From,
Pavar.

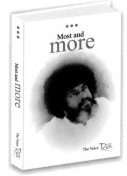

Published by **FROZEN THOUGHTS**
3, 3rd Cross Road, R A Puram,
Chennai, Tamil Nadu, India.
books@frozenthoughts.com
www.frozenthoughts.com

Printed at Srinivas Fine Arts (P) Ltd,
Keelathiruthangal, Sivakasi,
Tamil Nadu
Web Site : www.srinivasfinearts.com

©2011

Most and more
ISBN 978-81-9038-161-1

First Edition: 11.11.11
Copies Printed - 20,000 copies

• • •

In the infinite of time and space, it is only providential that you found me and I found you. The very fact that you are holding me, your life is on the threshold of a breakthrough.

I am made up of stories and I express myself through Avyakta, meaning the unmanifested. However, in my stories, Avyakta manifests as many Avatars to empower you to design your own destiny of Holistic Abundance.

Let that Cosmic presence, through me, radiate the insights that you truly deserve. Let me in...

My name is

most and more

The Voice *Rā*

Table of Contents

Table of Contents

• • •

What do you want to be? Somebody or anybody?

Make the decision right now. Do you want to be just anybody in life, or do you want to be somebody in life? If you want to be just anybody in life, then merge with the crowd. Get lost in the crowd. However, if you want to be somebody in life, then stand up and be counted. If you live like everybody, you will become like everybody. If you don't want to be like everybody, then you have to do what nobody has done. Walk a different path and you'll create a new destination for yourself.

He couldn't stop smiling. There was overflowing happiness. Two hours from now would be very special moments for him. Anticipation filled the air. Avyakta was boarding the flight at Chennai. He would be in Pune a couple of hours from now, to be received by a man who has had one of the greatest influences on his life.

Memories of the 'firsts' are always special and they enjoy a very special place in all our hearts. Pune was Avyakta's first experience away from home.

Most and more

Pune gave him his first job. He earned his first salary at Pune. He bought his first gift for his parents and brother from Pune. It was Pune that opened the doors to what eventually turned out to be an illustrious career for Avyakta. Pune had given a series of 'firsts' to Avyakta. In many ways, Pune was a home away from home for Avyakta. Avyakta was extremely ecstatic as he boarded the flight; it didn't seem as if he was going to just another city. It seemed like he had been given a multi-entry visa to heaven with all the tickets paid for.

From where to where, Avyakta wondered. He recalled his first journey to Pune by train in a second class compartment. Having paid Rs.80 on the ticket, all he was left with in his pocket when he went to Pune for the first time was Rs.20. All he had was three sets of clothes and a pair of oversized shoes borrowed from his cousin that had to be stuffed in the front with old newspapers. Avyakta's family was in dire straits and being the eldest son, Avyakta decided to bear the cross of his family when he was barely 19 and still in the final year of his graduation. He was on his way to take up a job at a software training institute.

Here he was a decade later, sitting in an aircraft, where his airfare was actually more than his annual take-home pay then. So much had changed. Actually, everything had changed. Why is the man whom

Avyakta is going to meet in Pune so special? Peter was Avyakta's first boss. Avyakta used to tell his friends, "I went to Pune as a boy and Peter made me a man. When I first met Peter, I was an unseasoned, unimpressive, unsystematic employee and he made me a seasoned, impressive, systematic, organised and mature professional. I am Peter's creation."

Avyakta was still an adolescent when he started his career. He allowed himself to be distracted by the girls who attended classes at the institute. He used to frequently bunk office and go for movies. He always had a justification for the compromises he made at his work. He was angry at life, for he believed that life had truncated his teens a little too early by dumping responsibilities on his young shoulders. He was frustrated that the joy of youth had been snatched away from him. Circumstances had driven him to take up a job, but his heart was constantly rebelling. He felt he hadn't been allowed to be a 19-year-old.

As providence would have it, Avyakta was working for Peter - a strict disciplinarian, a perfectionist and a very demanding manager. Peter had started earning for his family when he was fifteen and hence had no sympathy for the 19-year-old. Finding it difficult to cope with Peter's demands, Avyakta decided to resign and get back home.

Most and more

Holding Avyakta's resignation letter in his hand, Peter told Avyakta, "I will not accept this resignation till I have a personal conversation with you. Office isn't the place for a personal discussion; no matter how much I try, you will not open up. You will see me only as a manager talking to you with some ulterior motive. Let's meet at Boat Club this evening."

On his way to Boat Club that evening, Avyakta kept telling himself, "Don't let Peter manipulate your thoughts. Stand your ground. Don't give in. Be firm. If you want to enjoy life, you have to leave Pune and return home. Whatever be the demands of the family, this is the age to chill out, not the age to be burdened with responsibilities."

In spite of Avyakta's reluctance to have that evening meeting, Peter made that evening the defining moment of Avyakta's life. Once at Boat Club, they occupied a bench by the river, each holding a plate of *bhel*. Looking into Avyakta's eyes, Peter said, "With our relationship being barely a few months old, my easiest option would be to let you go. But by doing that, I will be allowing enormous human potential to let go of what it is capable of becoming. I can understand how a 19-year-old feels. I too have missed my youth and longed for it. But Avyakta, the big question is, 'Do you necessarily have to fit into the definition of a typical 19-year-old?' Movies, parties, hanging out, girls and guys, and chilling out - everybody does that. Why do you want to be one *among* the crowd? Why not be the one *above* the crowd? How many people are lucky enough to have an early start to their career? Avyakta, you've got a head start. Why not make the most of it? Don't lose this advantage."

By then, they had finished the *bhel*. Peter got up from the bench and suggested that they take a walk. As they started walking, Peter threw his arms around Avyakta and it meant so much to the 19-year-old. He felt respected. He felt an unexpressed affection in that gesture. He also felt an inexplicable sense of nervousness within. When someone you look up to in life relates with you as if you are a contemporary, then you experience slight shivers. Avyakta was going through exactly this. Nevertheless, Avyakta hoped that Peter wouldn't remove his hands from his shoulders. For Avyakta, the very experience of being with Peter was more overwhelming than his words.

Peter continued his empowering talk. "Make the decision right now. Do you want to be just *anybody* in life or do you want to be *somebody* in life? If you want to be just anybody in life, then quit your job and jump on the bandwagon. Merge with the crowd. Get lost in the crowd. However, if you want to be somebody in life, then stand up and be counted. If you live like everybody, you will become like everybody. If you don't want to be like everybody, then you have to do what nobody has done. Walk the path everybody walks, and you'll reach the destination everybody reaches. Walk a different path and you'll create a new destination for yourself. Avyakta, answer this simple question: 'Do you want to be a typical 19-year-old or do you want to be a 19-year-old who will be looked up to by other 19-year-olds'?"

Peter took his hand off Avyakta's shoulders. But now it didn't matter to Avyakta. Something within him had been awakened. There are certain moments in life that are too special and such moments happen only a few times in an entire lifetime. This was one such moment.

Seeing the determination in Avyakta's eyes, Peter continued, "There are just two options in life: 'Either subordinate your likes and dislikes to the purpose of your life; or, subordinate the purpose of your life to your likes and dislikes'. My boy, if you want to be somebody in life, if you want to stand above the crowd, if you want to be a 19-year-old who will be looked up to, then there is just one choice for you." Saying so, Peter pulled out Avyakta's resignation letter from his pocket, tore it up and tossed it into the next dustbin they crossed.

As the announcement of landing was made and passengers were asked to fasten their seat belts, Avyakta wiped the tears from his eyes and whispered to himself, "Thank you Peter. As a 29-year-old, I still keep reminding myself that I can either be a typical 29-year-old or a 29-year-old who will be looked up to by other 29-year-olds. Of course, it leaves me with no choice but to subordinate my likes and dislikes to the purpose of my life. Thank you so much Peter."

The flight landed in Pune, the place from which Avyakta's life took off.

Do you necessarily have to fit into the definition
of a typical 19-year-old?
There are just two options in life:
Either subordinate your likes and dislikes to the
purpose of your life; or, subordinate the purpose of
your life to your likes and dislikes.
If you want to be somebody in life,
if you want to stand above the crowd,
if you want to be the one who will be looked up to,
then there is just one choice.
So, do you want to be a typical 19-year-old
or do you want to be a 19-year-old who will be
looked up to by other 19-year-olds?

Most and more

• • •

Your future begins today

The pages you have already read in a book are mere build-up. The joy of the book is in the pages that you haven't read yet. Why write an imposition of a chapter from your past again and again and again... when you have the potential to write many more fresh chapters in the future? The glory of life is in the chapters to come. Save your future from the clutches of your past. Life should be a forward progression and not a backward regression. We cannot go back and make a fresh start, but we can begin now and create a fresh end. Draw a line to your past. Your yesterday was over yesterday. Your future begins today.

●●●

An evening away from greatness

We may be born in a middle-class family, but we can scale such heights in this lifetime that we can cause an industrial revolution. We may be born to illiterate parents, but we can die as a scholar of world repute. We may have been considered a misfit during our childhood days, but we can become role models for the future generation. What we are and what we have been has no bearing on what we can be. We can be, what we choose to be.

T he school had just won the finals of the national quiz championship. It was a very emotional moment for everyone in the school. They had lost the last year's finals by a whisker. Everyone in the school was in tears, then as well as now; just that the reasons were different. Nivya had been on both the teams. In the assembly, to celebrate the occasion, the Principal of the school invited Nivya to speak a few words. Nivya stood in front of the mike, first looked at all her fellow students, then turned towards the Principal and broke down. Many students and teachers could connect with what Nivya was going through and there were tears in the eyes of many. It wasn't a moment of triumph for Nivya alone; it was a moment of triumph for the whole school.

After composing herself, Nivya said, "I first thank our Principal for all her encouragement. She works as if her sole mission in life is to see each one of us reach the top in areas of our choice. I also thank my parents for the freedom they have given me to choose my extra-curricular activities, rather than imposing their 'will' on me. I will fail in my duty if I don't thank my teachers who have repeated this mantra to me time and again, 'Nivya, you can do it'. Often, they have shown greater faith in me than what I had in myself. I know how I felt last year after we had lost in the finals and I know how different it feels this year after this success. Above all other factors there is this one man who is responsible for this transformation. If now our school is in the national reckoning, it is all because of..." Nivya's eyes began to scan the crowd and stopped on spotting Avyakta.

Avyakta was a trainee who had joined the school only the previous year to teach Mathematics. Though not many teachers in that big ocean of over 250 teachers knew Avyakta by name, he was very popular amongst his students. It was not for the way he taught the subject but for all the other aspects of life that he discussed with them. Avyakta split his forty-minute period into thirty minutes for the subject and ten minutes to interact with his students and inspire them on various aspects of human dynamics. One of the reasons he was not very popular with the teaching faculty was that he was breaking away from conventional teaching methods, and they detested that. They screamed, "You are a novice. Don't be overenthusiastic and try too many things. All this doesn't work. You will not be able to complete the syllabus."

But then, think about it. Never has an expert ever changed a traditional system or revolutionised any system with groundbreaking methods. It is always people who work at the periphery of a system that look at it from a different perspective and bring about revolutionary changes. The cutting edge rarely comes from people who work at the core of a system, but always from people who work at the periphery of a system.

In a novice's mind, there are several possibilities. In an expert's mind, there are but a few. Avyakta was a novice when it came to teaching, and hence the possibilities of innovation. But then, teachers often do not like other teachers who are popular with students. Avyakta knew that his methods were right and that they would eventually be recognised by the school. So he continued to follow his heart.

Nivya, pointing towards Avyakta, said, "One of his ten-minute sessions made all the difference. Though I was back in school two days after the previous year's defeat, I was still finding it difficult to concentrate in class. I felt I had let the school down. This was written all over my face and he probably noticed it during one of the Maths periods. That day, Avyakta Sir made eye contact with me and with radiance in his eyes that I have never seen before said, 'Nivya, for all you know, you are just an evening away from greatness'. Then he turned to the class and added, 'In the process of climbing to the top in whatever you people choose to do, there are going to be moments of failure and defeat. Greatness of character does not lie in thinking positive when everything is going like a song, but in thinking positive when things are going deadly wrong'."

Nivya concluded, "The evening before this final I kept uttering to myself that I am just an evening away from greatness. Even as I went to sleep that night, somewhere subconsciously this chattering that I am just an evening away from greatness kept lingering.

So, on my own behalf and on behalf of the whole team, I dedicate this victory to Avyakta Sir."

Some ran towards Nivya to congratulate her and some ran towards Avyakta to congratulate him. As the celebrations were on, the Principal took over the mike and said, "Do Avyakta's ten-minute sessions make so much of a difference? I have never heard you speak Avyakta. Why don't you deliver one of your ten-minute sessions to the whole school? Let me also have the opportunity of listening to you." Blushing with embarrassment at the loud cheers, Avyakta shook hands with Nivya on the way and walked up to the podium. This was the first time he was facing such a large gathering. Avyakta had never before spoken on the mike. He stood before the mike, turned towards the Principal and as if to make a mockery of the opportunity provided, asked the Principal, "What should I speak?" He followed it up with an uneasy smile, shattering the image that Nivya had just created of him. One of the students from the assembly shrieked, "Come on, Avyakta Sir! You are just a speech away from greatness," and the whole assembly burst out laughing. The Principal encouraged him. "Go on Avyakta, go on."

As some of the teachers, who could not relish the adulation Avyakta was receiving, were beginning to experience sadistic satisfaction at the prospect of Avyakta's impending moment of humiliation, Avyakta closed his eyes and began.

"Visualise a chessboard with the pieces on it. In the first row are lined what are called the powers - a pair of rooks, a pair of bishops, a pair of knights, a king and a queen. In the second row are lined eight pieces - the pawns. Though we call the pieces in the first row as powers, they have one handicap. A rook can only be a rook till the very end of the game; a bishop, only a bishop; and a knight, only a knight. Whether you see them only as the rook, bishop and knight or, as an amateur chess player would call them, the elephant (rook), the camel (bishop) and the horse (knight)... it does not matter; but all the three so-called powers symbolise the lower forms of creation, animals, which are born to a nature, live within their nature and die to their nature. Though at birth most animals are functionally more capable than a human being, their curse is that they are limited by their nature. So are the so-called powers on the chessboard - the rook, the bishop and the knight."

At the prospect of something very new, very original that was emerging, the Principal adjusted the direction of her chair to face the podium. Some of the teachers, who had been standing until then, waiting for the assembly to get over, were now looking for empty seats to occupy. Nivya was all smiles... in fact, her face was buried in her smile. She was worshipping her Avyakta Sir. To her, it was just her Avyakta Sir and she... she was oblivious to everything else in the assembly.

Avyakta, now totally in a zone, was flowing with spontaneity. "Now, what about the other two pieces - the king and the queen? Like what Shakespeare said: 'Some are born great, some achieve greatness, and some have greatness thrust upon them.' The 'king' represents, in Shakespeare's parlance, those that are 'born great'. The 'queen' represents those that have 'greatness thrust upon them'. The queen, by virtue of being the king's wife, has greatness thrust upon her. Of course, in cases like the Queen of Great Britain, the reverse is true. However, even the pieces of the king and the queen have the same handicap of being born to a nature, living within that nature and finally dying to that nature."

Avyakta, who had been speaking with his eyes closed until this point, opened them. He continued in a booming voice. "Now let us focus on the pawns. To me, they represent what Shakespeare referred to as those that 'achieve greatness'. Every pawn is just six moves away from becoming the queen - the most

Most and more

powerful piece on the board. The pawn actually represents the common man, you and me:... though we are born to a nature, we are bestowed with the ability to transcend our nature. We may be born in a middle-class family, but we can scale such heights in this lifetime by bringing about an industrial revolution. We may be born to illiterate parents, but we can die as a world-renowned scholar. We may have been considered a misfit during childhood, but we can become role models for future generations. What we are and what we have been has no bearing on what we can become. We alone can proclaim, even on the days we have failed - 'so what, we are just an evening away from greatness'. Like the pawns, we are born to a nature, but do not have to die to the same nature. We are, like the pawns, just a few moves away from greatness."

Avyakta then bowed down to the Principal and moved away from the podium. There was a standing ovation and the Principal stepped forward and shook hands with Avyakta. Nivya ran towards Avyakta and said, "Thank you so much, Sir." Avyakta placed his hand on Nivya's head, as if to bless her, and said, "I am proud of you. Wishing you most and more..." and blushing with embarrassment, rushed to the staffroom.

A few weeks later, in one of the leading garment showrooms, Avyakta discovered that one of the leading

T-shirt manufacturers had stolen his messages and manufactured T-shirts with these messages printed on them: 'An evening away from greatness'. Another T-Shirt had an illustration of a chessboard and a pawn sporting a thick moustache, saying 'Six moves away from greatness'. Avyakta held the T-shirt in his hands, laughed, and then murmured, "Why did they put a moustache on the pawn? My pawns are not necessarily men... but women too."

Never has an expert ever changed
a traditional system or revolutionised
any system with groundbreaking methods.
It is always people who work
at the periphery of a system that look at it
from a different perspective and bring about
revolutionary changes. The cutting edge
rarely comes from people who work
at the core of a system, but always from people
who work at the periphery of a system.
In a novice's mind, there are several possibilities.
In an expert's mind, there are but a few.

Most and more

• • •

Be loyal to the chair

When the head of an organisation is not loyal to his chair, it jeopardises the whole organisation; he becomes a bottleneck to organisational growth. Only when he is loyal to the responsibilities of the chair, he will be able to steer the company into progress. From that chair, he should not be focussing on petty issues or the daily crises in the organisation. Then the head of the organisation becomes the most expensive clerk in the company. Instead, the head of an organisation is expected to develop a vision for the future, discuss tie-ups and collaborations, build organisational culture, create second line of operations, look into diversifications and most importantly ensure that the systems are in place. The primary responsibility is to make the organisation ready for the future.

I deserve Abundance

Your thoughts create your reality. You get what you focus on. That which you focus on is what you attract towards yourself. You see in any situation what you expect to see. You should focus on 'what you want' and not on 'what you do not want'. The cardinal rule is I get exactly what I focus on. So, choose to focus on 'Personal Abundance'.

I t was a Friday evening, and five men, all in their late thirties, had decided on a reunion at Gandhi Beach in Chennai. They had graduated together in the early eighties and had been very close to each other during their times in college. All of them had aspired to do their Engineering, but ended up (ended down!!!) in an Arts College. In fact, it was this sense of defeat that had brought the five of them together. They had similar tales to share on the very first day of college and had thus struck a chord with each other. Three of them were brilliant at academics; another, though average in academics had an outstanding personality and the fifth, Avyakta, had come to college because there was a college to come to. Neither the Professors nor his own classmates had ever thought that Avyakta would complete his graduation. The five of them were meeting again after eighteen years.

Time brings all of us to a stage in life when our own past seems like someone else's life. Eighteen years in the life of a progressing individual is like eternity. So much had changed from the reckless boys they were to the responsible men they had become; from being a matter of concern to their parents to now being concerned about the future of their children; indeed, so much had changed.

All four of them, except Avyakta, had pursued their master's; two of them had, in fact, completed double postgraduate degrees. Of course, right from their college days, every time the five of them were referred to, the phrase 'except Avyakta', was a common refrain. Two of them were software professionals and had settled in the USA; one had joined the public sector and the other, a private enterprise. All of them, except Avyakta, had well-paid jobs and owned an apartment. By social standards, for a middle-class family, they were all well settled.

Though four of them had anticipated reaching such a stage in their lives, they were surprised by the inconceivable growth of Avyakta. Avyakta had founded three organisations, and all of them were flourishing. He was living a swanky lifestyle.

The four of them were stunned by Avyakta's growth because they were convinced that Avyakta's IQ was below average. How often we give up on people because of this number-tag on human intelligence! They were convinced that he had no special talent, no special capabilities; there was nothing special at all about him. They had forgotten a very special quality that Avyakta always possessed; perhaps eighteen years had caused a memory lapse in them. When all of them were learning typewriting and shorthand during college days, Avyakta had refused to learn those skills saying, "One day I will have a secretary who will possess these skills." When all of them appeared for the Bank Services exams, Avyakta had refused to even buy the application form saying, "I do not belong to the other side of the counter. I can't see myself there. One day, bankers will come to me." When all of them encouraged him to go in for his postgraduate degree, at least through correspondence, he stated with aplomb, "I will not be a postgraduate, but I will have many postgraduates working for me one day."

Yet, Avyakta, like his name, was very unique. He was very different from the herd. Even as a schoolboy, Avyakta used to tell his friends, "Being born in a middle-class family is a consequence, but to ensure one does not die in a middle-class family is a matter of choice." While his friends in the colony used to wonder which cricket team to join, Avyakta used to ponder on how to start a cricket team so that it could be run on his terms. He used to tell his parents, "If someone has to lead, then it might as well be me."

Avyakta's secret, real talent and magic wand was that he refused to accept anything but the best from life, even at the level of thought. Like Disraeli puts it, "Life is too short to be little," Avyakta believed that a life of abundance was his birthright. In a world that never believes anything unless it sees it, Avyakta's rationale was, "What you believe in, you will see." He believed in a future filled with abundance and that became his reality. His friends believed in a future of adequacy and that became their reality. Avyakta, who could not get the better of his friends in most aspects, scored over them in the all-important aspect of life - his ability to think BIG. Rain fills the size of your vessel. Whether your life will be filled with scarcity, abundance or adequacy depends on the size of your thinking.

As if they had all been waiting for the clock at the beach to strike six times, they all arrived about the same time. Amid laughter and high-fives and hugs, the five of them had some true and some exaggerated stories to share. After about three hours, Avyakta said that he had to leave, as his wife and children would be waiting for him.

After passing a few sarcastic comments about Avyakta in specific, and marriage in general, the four of them said they would stay back for some more time and asked Avyakta to leave, if he choose to. Avyakta signed off by giving each one of them a parting hug.

After Avyakta left, the four friends noticed that he had left behind his personal organiser. Though one of them opted to catch up with Avyakta and hand it over to him, the other three were consumed with inquisitiveness to know what information it held. Majority prevailed and they converged like a litter of newborn puppies craving for the warmth of each other's body. A set of eight eyes peered into the personal organiser. They had scanned through the diary section, then the section on birthdays and anniversaries and then the section on contact addresses and phone numbers... and then... an add-on section, which Avyakta in his own handwriting had titled, 'The keys to my personal abundance'. This section of the personal organiser was full of snippets of wisdom. Neither of the four were sure whether this wisdom had been collected from other great men or whether they were experiential realisations born out of the life that had unfolded for Avyakta! Oh, the source hardly mattered. They were secrets of Avyakta's abundance and that was important for all of them.

Most and more

On the very first page they found this bold inscription in red ink, "I know 'THERE IS A WAY'."

Page after page was filled with words of wisdom that were worth a lifetime of search and research. After every page, they looked at each other, smiling sometimes but mostly nodding their heads in agreement. Soon the playful expressions had vanished from their faces and a sense of learning had engulfed them. They read,

1. When I believe that 'I can do it' and really believe in it, then the 'how to do it' automatically unfolds. Believing something can be done sets the mind in motion to find a way to do it.

2. My thoughts create my reality. I get what I focus on. That which I focus on is what I attract towards myself. You see in any situation what you expect to see. If there is something I hate, it is because I am focusing on it. If there is love, it is because I am focusing on it. If someone is driving me nuts, it is because I am focusing on him. I should focus on 'what I am FOR' and not on 'what I am AGAINST'. The cardinal rule is I get exactly what I focus on. Every book, every philosopher and every great thinker of the world has eventually led me to exactly the same conclusion. So I have chosen to focus on 'My personal abundance'.

3. Abundance is just manifested energy. If I can take care of my energy levels, my abundance will be taken care of. Nothing will be mine unless I am convinced that it belongs to me. I deserve abundance. I am not going to go in search of abundance but I will make abundance flow into my life. I deserve most and more...

4. People are basically a product of their psychological environment. We are conditioned by the thinking of those around us. 'Scarcity' thinkers are leading us to think of scarcity rather than abundance. People who say 'it cannot be done' are generally unsuccessful people; they are strictly average or at best mediocre in terms of accomplishment. It is a notable fact that people with mediocre accomplishments are quick to explain why they haven't, why they don't, why they can't and why they aren't. Rather than mingling with these people who suffer from 'tradition paralysis', I will rub shoulders with people who are 'abundant minded'. I will use every brick of negativity that is thrown at me only as another stepping-stone to build my castle. After all, I am on this planet to build my castle, not my grave.

5. On my road to abundance I may face challenges, failures and setbacks. Yet, I will never feel defeated.

If I were driving down a road and came upon a 'road closed' sign, would I sit in my car until the work gets completed on the road or would I return home? Neither! The 'road closed' sign simply means that I cannot go where I want to go on this particular road. My path may change... my destination never will.

6. I will respect everyone. I will learn from everyone. I will observe everyone. I will study everyone's life. However, in the materialistic realm, I will worship no man. I believe that I can go beyond and will surpass everyone. I will consciously shun the attitude of being the second best. I am not here to be a second-hand human being. In all that I do, the space for No.1 already has my name engraved on it. I just need to go for it and discover it.

7. No matter how little I have, I am rich if I am grateful. No matter how much I have, I am poor if I am not grateful. I will not only be grateful for what I have, but will also always give a portion of what I have to the world around me. I will consistently experience myself as a giver. It is through giving that I will create this neuro-association in my mind that I have more than enough and my mind will convert it into reality. Gratitude and giving are ways of creating abundance.

The four of them were spellbound as they closed the personal organiser, glanced at each other and looked up. To their shock, they saw Avyakta standing about five feet away, his hands folded across his chest, sporting a broad smile. Stuttering and stammering, they said, "Sorry! We just thought..." Avyakta interrupted and said, "I have no secrets in my life... certainly not with my friends. Like my personal organiser, I am also an open book. If you guys need it, keep those pages with you. I don't need those pages anymore... those dictums are etched into every cell of my system." Saying so, he removed the pages from his organiser and handed them over to his friends.

Then he added, "A day comes when the caterpillar decides not to remain a caterpillar anymore. So it goes into a cocoon to develop wings, and becomes a butterfly. One day, the caterpillar in me just decided to turn into a butterfly. I gave up 'scarcity thinking' and embraced the 'abundance mentality'. Everything else followed. I had answers to 'Why I need abundance', and as a reward life unfolded the 'How'. I am saying this to you since I know the four of you so personally. Eighteen years ago, when all of us were just caterpillars, the four of you were much better than me. It's just that none of you ever decided to turn into a butterfly. Even if you decide now, starting today, every day of your life will unfold miracles of abundance. Wishing you guys most and more…"

As Avyakta began to walk, he shouted, "Any dream is achievable! There are no limits…" Though it was well beyond 10.00 p.m., it seemed as though the sun never sets when people like Avyakta are around.

I will respect everyone.
I will learn from everyone.
I will observe everyone.
I will study everyone's life.
However, in the materialistic realm,
I will worship no man.
I believe that I can go beyond
and will surpass everyone.
I will consciously shun
the attitude of being the second best.
I am not here to be a second-hand human being.
In all that I do, the space for No.1
already has my name engraved on it.
I just need to go for it and discover it.
Nothing will be mine unless I am convinced
that it belongs to me. I deserve abundance.
I am not going to go in search of abundance
but I will make abundance flow into my life.

Experience... what is it?

It is not enough that you improve the quality of your communication with the world outside. In fact, it is even more important that you improve the quality of your communication with yourself. What you tell the world and what the world tells you make a small difference to you. However, what you keep telling yourself makes all the difference to you.

P ointing to Aldous Huxley's quote, "Experience is not what happens to you. It is what you do with what happens to you," Suj, Avyakta's wife, sought clarification from him.

It is so heartening when your spouse can also be your intellectual companion. People go through intellectual loneliness. They wish to share their comprehensions and contemplations of life, but don't find people interested in such intellectual contemplations. There is a different depth and quality to the relationships when husband and wife, parents and children, friends, siblings, colleagues not only discuss the day-to-day issues, but also enquire into the deeper and higher issues of life. When we think

Most and more

together, when we agree to disagree, when we understand that beyond my way and your way there can be a third way, the possibilities are limitless. Suj and Avyakta enjoyed their moments of intellectual exploration. In the intellectual sense, one plus one is always greater than two.

"What does Huxley imply when he says experience is what you do with what happens to you?" enquired Suj.

"I tell you I will be home by eight, but land up at nine. This is just an event of a husband ending up being late by an hour. You process that as 'I have taken you for granted' and 'I no more have respect for you'. Your mind questions, 'Will he do this if it was a meeting with his Chairman?' and it also concludes 'It is time to tell him that I am not a doormat'. And the event is just that I landed up an hour late. But the interpretation of the event by your mind is that I don't respect you and I have taken you for granted. That isn't necessarily the reality. It is only your perception of reality. It is your interpretation of reality. That's what Huxley meant when he said 'it is what you do with what happens to you'," retorted Avyakta.

Suj poked Avyakta with her index finger and said with a smile, "You simply can't explain anything without making a dig at me. Hey, don't talk as if you are some angel of a man! When I give you a feedback with a genuine intent to help you to improve, you interpret it as 'I am finding fault with you all the time' and you get agitated. I said the same things in the initial months of our marriage, and you used to say, 'I am so lucky to have you in my life. You always help me to improve'. I say the same things to you now. But, then I was an angel and now I am a devil." Of course, by the last sentence, the smile on Suj's face had already vanished.

In the presence of love, events are interpreted differently. When ego pops its head, events are interpreted differently. If it is a stranger, the event is interpreted differently. If it is a relative then the interpretation is different. If it is men from that community, then the interpretation is different. If they are from that linguistic background, then there is a different generalisation for them.

Like the icons on a desktop, we hold icons for every person in our head. Some icons represent good people, some wonderful people, some not so good, some we cannot even stand, some the worst kind, and so on... These icons serve as the spectacles through which we perceive people and accordingly interpret what they do and what they do not do. When she is a good person in our head, then even a wrong from her is nullified and accepted. When he is a bad person in our head, then even a right from him is negated and overlooked. Essentially, whether they are good or bad in our head is completely different from the actual reality. That's why, the same person is perceived as a devil by one and an angel by another. What Gandhi is in your head and what Gandhi was in Godse's head are independent of what Gandhi actually was. What you see in Christ is not what Pilate saw in him. How true! The person need not change; when the icon we hold for the person in our head changes, it changes the relationship completely, positively or negatively.

"Let us not bring in our personal emotions into this discussion and tarnish the whole enquiry," clarified Avyakta. "What you are asking is important. Aldous Huxley has revealed a great insight."

Suj walked into her open-kitchen and started preparing tea. Avyakta followed. There were two things he couldn't resist in life - Suj and her tea. Avyakta sat on the kitchen counter. He continued, "So, what happens to us is an event. How we process, perceive and interpret that event becomes our experience. So, the same event becomes a different experience for different people, depending on how they process, perceive and interpret it. Being pushed out of the train at Pietermaritzburg railway station in South Africa was an event. Gandhi could have gone into depression. However, the way he chose to process, perceive and interpret that event turned out to be a turning point, not only for him but also for a great nation." Avyakta added with laughter, "The whole British empire must be cursing that one white man... if only he had allowed Gandhi to continue to travel in the first-class compartment!"

Suj intervened, "It is even more evident in the context of all these understandings that more than the problem, it is my reaction to the problem that hurts me more. More than the calamity, it is my fear of the calamity that hurts me more. More than your actions, it is how I process, perceive and interpret your action that has a bearing on the relationship; it also has a bearing on my peace of mind. The way I see the problem is the problem. The way I see the problem can also be my solution. If I see it as a failure, it is a failure. Instead, if I see failure as a mere outcome with a feedback, I can improve with every experience. Success has its share of lessons and so do failures. In fact, what failures can teach, success cannot; and what success can teach, failures cannot. Good times, bad times or filtering times are all matters of perceptions. I can choose to perceive any event the way I want. So, progress and stagnation are just the result and effect of how I choose to process the events of my life." She then snapped, "Thank your stars Avyakta, in spite of you, our relationship has progressed because I have interpreted all your actions as your expressions of love, irrespective of what your intent might have been."

The tea was ready. Sipping his tea, Avyakta explained, "In the context of love, sarcasm induces humour. In the context of ego, sarcasm induces hurt. This is what they should have meant when they said 'It is *Maya*... just an illusion'. After all, we are not dealing with reality, but only with perceived reality. We are actually not facing situations, but our interpretation of the situations. It is not what you are, but it is what I think of you that has a bearing on my relationship with you. So, even God needn't be a reality. As long as I can hold an icon of devotion, surrender and faith for that perceived reality, it works in my favour."

Avyakta concluded, "So, it is not enough that you improve the quality of your communication with the world outside. In fact, it is even more important that you improve the quality of your communication with yourself. What you tell the world and what the world tells you make a small difference to you. However, what you keep telling yourself makes all the difference to you. What happens to you is not in your control. But, how you process what happens to you is completely in your control. And in controlling that, you control your whole life. So, if everything about your life has to change, all you have to do is to change the icons you hold in your head and also control what you take into your head."

Suj remarked, "Events are God's responsibility. Experiences are man's responsibility."

How true... we share the same world, and yet, we experience our own worlds. Two men saw through the prison bars. One saw the mud. The other saw the stars.

Avyakta and Suj embraced each other. What this embrace meant to each of them will ever remain a secret to the other. Who will ever know how they perceived it?

What happens to us is an event.
How we process, perceive and interpret
that event becomes our experience.
Being pushed out of the train at Pietermaritzburg
railway station in South Africa was an event.
Gandhi could have gone into depression.
However, the way he chose to process, perceive
and interpret that event became a turning point,
not only for him but also for a great nation.

●●●

Your life is your responsibility

On the road, it is never the question of whose mistake; but, it is the question of whose life! On the road, if you want to be alive YOU have to make the adjustments. The responsibility of 'not hitting' and 'not being hit', both are yours and yours alone. Blaming makes no sense. Similarly, in the road called life, in dealing with the traffic called relationships, it is not the question of whose mistake, but it is the question of whose life. In relationships too, if you want happiness, YOU have to make the adjustments. Here too, blaming makes no sense. Your life is your responsibility.

An opportunist in thinking

Anybody can think positive when everything is going right. It's when things are not going right that you need to be in the right frame of mind. After all, with the power of your thoughts, you can 'will' almost anything to happen. Hence, with the power of your thoughts, you can set anything right. Getting our thinking right is the sure-fire way of getting our life right. It is even more important to think right, when things are going wrong.

She was an angel. That's how Avyakta had brought her up in life. And that's how she had turned out to be. As you sow, so you reap. The effect is nothing but the cause itself in a different form. Every child is a reflection of the parenting that's gone in. She was daddied (why mothered and not daddied - let's expand our vocabulary to do justice to dads) like an angel and she grew up to be an angel.

To her, her dad was her lifeline. Whenever she felt insecure, she would rest her head on her dad's lap. Her dad's lap was her security blanket. Her dad's fingers running through her hair always took her

---

Most and more

into a state of trance. She would become oblivious of the world around. She would completely believe anything he told her in that state. It was almost like hypnosis. Her dad was everything to her. To her, anything and everything seemed possible with Avyakta, her dad, in her life.

That evening, the angel was again gently resting her head on Avyakta's lap. Uncertainties and insecurities are part of growing years. When people intellectualise their problems, you can intellectualise your solutions too. However, when people are emotional about their problems, it isn't the time to talk solutions; it is time for protective love. It is time to make the other person feel secure with your protective love. The need of the hour was an unspoken assurance, through gestures and touch, "I understand. I am with you. I am there for you. Daddy will take care."

Avyakta noticed two lines of tears rolling down his daughter's cheeks. She wasn't speaking, and hence this wasn't the time to speak. Avyakta is just a casual singer, but love cares not for the grammar of singing. Avyakta sang the lullaby wanting his daughter to go to sleep. "Goodnight my angel, time to close your eyes and save these questions for another day. I think I know what you've been asking me. I think you know what I've been trying to say. I promise I will never leave you and you should always know, wherever you may go, no matter where you are, I never will be far away. Goodnight my angel, now it's time to dream and dream how wonderful your life will be. Someday we'll all be gone, but lullabies go on and on... That's how you and I will be."

The tears had stopped. The little one tightened her grip; a gesture that suggested, "Speak Dad, speak! I want to listen to you." Still running his fingers through her hair, Avyakta said, "Hey my little angel, anybody can think positive when everything is going right. It's when things are not going right that you need to be in the right frame of mind. After all, with the power of your thoughts, you can 'will' almost anything to happen. Hence, with the power of your thoughts, you can set anything right. Getting our thinking right is the sure-fire way of getting our life right. It is even more important to think right, when things are going wrong."

There was strength in the content, but gentleness in the tone of voice. When people feel delicate and fragile, the voice that attempts to heal them needs to be soothing. Over-confidence in the voice during such moments will only make them breakdown further. There was love and affection in the touch, in the voice and even in the breathing.

Most and more

The eyes were still closed, but the eyeballs were moving. She wasn't ready to sleep now, as she was ready to be awakened. Avyakta said, "One of the universal laws of life is; 'Like begets like; like attracts like'. By the thoughts you hold most dominant in your mind, you will draw more and more of similar thoughts into your mind. Things being a mere manifestation of thoughts, your most dominant thoughts will manifest in your life. So, whenever we go through tough times in life or when life is not treating us the way we want to be treated, we so easily slip into negative thinking. We develop the spectacles through which everything seems wrong. The problem with this mentality is that the negative thoughts that you are currently holding in your mind will begin to draw more and more of similar negative thoughts and that will become your most dominant thought pattern. When that becomes your most dominant thought pattern that is exactly what you will keep drawing into your life. That's why when things begin to go wrong, so much more goes wrong. When life throws you into tough times, everything turns out to be tough. It happens this way because of the thinking trap we fall into. When everything you think is negative, everything that happens obviously turns out to be negative. Revolution is to go into a vicious cycle and evolution is to come out of that cycle. Hey little one, come out of the vicious cycle of your thought patterns."

She altered her position to make herself more comfortable. She shook her head as if to ask "How?" Avyakta smiled, whacked her lightly on the head and continued, "Learn from your dad. Have you noticed that I am a big opportunist in thinking? I always control the direction of my mind and think only what I want to think. When my present isn't what I want it to be, I take the time to recall the glorious past I have had. Sometimes in relationships, when the present is not all that smooth and there is no past in the relationship, I focus my mind on the future of the relationship and dream how wonderful it will turn out to be. In situations where neither the past, nor the present, nor the future seem too promising, I search for people who have gone through what I am going through, who have come out smelling of roses, and focus my mind on them. I am an opportunist when it comes to my thinking. I only think what I want to think. Hence, I end up drawing into my life only what I want in my life. After all, like begets like. Control the direction of your thinking and always manage to hold positive thoughts as your most dominant thoughts, and see how you navigate through life."

To the girl who got up and sat, Avyakta said, "I practice the same even with people. I search for something positive in every person I have been acquainted with, either qualities or incidents, and hold that as my most dominant thought whenever I meet them or think of them. No wonder I have always drawn such wonderful people into my life! Like begets like. Even when I am sick, I either recall the days I have been healthy or visualise a healthier future and process that more than the present sickness. No wonder I have not missed a single working day on account of sickness ever in my entire career. My rate of recovery astounds even doctors."

"However, a word of caution my child," Avyakta added, "Since we have to be prepared for all possible contingencies in life, while planning projects and while introspecting life, by decision, wear the black hat and think what can be negative, what could have been overlooked, what can go wrong, what is bad. Only for contemplation and analysis, by choice, examine the negative so that you can take precautions to counter the negative. Anticipating rains and carrying an umbrella is not negative thinking. It is just proper contingency planning. However, after introspection when you are back in the present continuous, get back to being an incorrigible positive thinker. Use your mind well and 'will' your life."

Almost as a parting question, Avyakta asked, "By the way, what is bothering you?" It seems angels don't talk. The little one was in no mood to speak.

She simply leaned over and hugged her dad, as if to say, "Dad, you plus me is enough, more than enough. I can and I will be able to do anything; handle anything."

Still lost in the embrace, Avyakta whispered a few lines from the lullaby again, "Goodnight my angel, now it's time to dream and dream how wonderful your life will be... I promise I will never leave you." This time there were four lines of tears. Both the angel and the God of the angel, Avyakta, were in tears. Why? Hmmm... if you know why, then you will not cry.

Whenever we go through tough times, we so easily slip into negative thinking.
The problem with this mentality is that your mind will begin to draw more and more of similar negative thoughts. That's why when things begin to go wrong, so much more goes wrong.
I am an opportunist when it comes to my thinking.
I only think what I want to think. Hence,
I end up drawing into my life only what I want in my life. After all, like begets like. Control the direction of your thinking and always manage to hold positive thoughts as your most dominant thoughts, and see how you navigate through life.

Most and more

•••

Do you have the right questions?

Our intelligence has an inherent compulsion to answer any question that is posed to it, either by you or by the world. So, choose your questions and direct your intelligence in constructive ways. In fact, all inventions and discoveries begin with a question. It doesn't matter if you don't have all the answers. Someone will provide you the answers. Answers will come from 'Out of the Blue'. What truly matters is, do you have the right questions? Ask and you shall receive.

● ● ●

Is there a way to measure growth?

Parents, relatives, teachers, and society work together in the making of a man. A lot of investment goes into the making of a man. Consequently, every man has a moral responsibility to live a life worthy of his potential. Is there a way to know if man is doing justice to his potential or not?

When you study in the same school for 14 years, from your lower kindergarten to the twelfth standard, your school becomes your second home. Jai would be passing out of school this year. From teachers to students everybody knew that Jai has no competition for the most coveted 'The Best Outgoing Student' award. The school day function was this evening, and this evening was going to be Jai's evening.

We all become what we become in life because someone believed in us much before we began to believe in ourselves. That someone was Avyakta for Jai.

Most and more

The student-teacher chemistry is a mystery. We never know when it will happen, with whom it will happen and why it happens. But as and when it does happen, miraculous transformations happen. Jai and Avyakta shared such chemistry. The student-teacher chemistry just clicked. In discovering Avyakta, Jai discovered himself. Avyakta saw something in Jai and hence began to work on Jai. Jai would so often proudly proclaim, "I'm my teacher's product."

Jai came a little too early to school that evening. He went in search of Avyakta from one staffroom to another. When he approached the ninth standard block, he heard Avyakta's voice coming from one of the staffrooms. Avyakta was in conversation with one of his old students. The 'hero' of the evening waited outside, but he could clearly hear the conversation. The old student belonged to the first batch of Avyakta's students, and had passed out from school almost two decades ago. Sharing his success story with the 'potter' behind the 'pot', he spoke about how he had done 18 crores the previous year, what his future plans were, his family life, and some memories of his good old school days. He was attempting to give a complete picture to Avyakta. Needless to say, Jai's imagination ran wild thinking what he would be sharing with Avyakta when he would meet him 20 years later.

The old student hugged Avyakta before taking leave. When Jai entered the staffroom, Avyakta was beaming from ear to ear. More than your own success, the success of those you create is always dearer to you. In a way, this was Jai's evening. In a way this was also Avyakta's evening. Avyakta, a man with an eye for detail, asked, "Have you prepared your speech of acceptance?" Jai replied, "Expecting this question from you I've already prepared my speech of acceptance."

"Sir, feed my curiosity," Jai said, "I happened to overhear the conversation between you and your old student. What does it mean to you, Sir, when students you have created do so well in life? I mean, how do you take it? I know what teaching means to you. Yet, do you go through thoughts like, while I have remained a teacher, the world I have created has moved ahead. No doubt you have been a ladder for all the leaders you have created, but don't you feel, Sir, that you have remained where you were? Can I have some clarity, Sir, on what goes on inside Avyakta Sir's head?"

Anything from his wonder boy made Avyakta smile. He asked Jai to take a seat. He glanced at the clock; there was at least another half hour to go. Avyakta said, "The 'cause' doesn't compare itself with the 'effect'. Why will parents compare their success with their children's; why would a teacher evaluate his life relative to that of a student; why will a potter be affected by the adulation his pot gets? Gardeners know that the trees they create will outlive them. Teachers, potters, gardeners... they are creators. Personally, there has never ever been even a slightest thought in that direction of comparing my life with that of my students. Only when you asked this question did I realise that you can also look at things that way. In fact, it will be *adharma* for a teacher to compare himself with his students. My *dharma* is to create, and create I shall as a teacher... twenty years ago it was him, today it is you, and tomorrow it will be someone else. A creator never compares himself with his creation."

Jai smiled in return and said, "That's what makes you who you are. That's why a student comes back to you twenty years later and shares his success story with you. I feel so blessed to have been created by you. I will also earn in crores and come back to share my success story with you, Sir."

"Nevertheless," Avyakta clarified, "Jai, you should remember one thing. Money is a wonderful by-product and a very poor point-of-focus. When your work becomes your self-expression, money comes in search of you as a natural by-product. It cannot be the other way around, where money is the point-of-focus and work is only a means to it. People who work purely for the sake of money may know success, but they will never know what it is to be Happily Successful. When the process of creation drives you, the creation-fee that life pays you for what you create is money. And Jai, prosperity is a fallacy. Even with crores, you are always poorer than someone else; even with thousands, you are always richer than somebody else. It is so relative. He who isn't happy with what he has will never be happy no matter how much more he has. So, live to create."

"Sure Sir," agreed Jai. "But, one last question." Both of them glanced at the clock. Avyakta nodded. Jai asked, "If it is not money, then how do I measure my growth?"

"Good question," Avyakta acknowledged. "All your life, make yourself accountable to these three questions. They are,

1. Am I doing justice to my potential?

2. Year after year, in how many more lives am I becoming useful?

3. Day by day, am I living my life in ways by which I am moving closer and closer to my god?

Firstly, no matter how much you accomplish in life, keep asking yourself, 'Am I doing justice to my potential?'

Man was created to create. Man was designed to design his life. The very process of birth, and then through parents, relatives, teachers, and society - a lot of investment has gone into the making of a man. As a result, every man has a moral responsibility to live a life worthy of his potential. Success is not what you achieve compared to others, but what you achieve compared to what you are capable of. And what you are capable of is defined by the infinite potential sleeping within you."

Avyakta continued, "Now the question is, 'How will I know if I am doing justice to my potential?' There comes the second question: Year after year, in how many more lives am I becoming useful? Even a cow, a bull, a parrot feeds a family of humans. It would be a shame to live a life of mediocrity, a life merely for *me, mine and myself.* Measure your success by the usefulness of your life. None of us are useless. Just that, we are used less."

"And finally," Avyakta concluded, "we are living in times when people believe even murder is okay to produce results. No, it is not okay! Without ethical and moral accountability, as I said earlier, success may be possible, but being happily successful is not. Mark 10:25 states, 'It is easier for a camel to go through the eye of a needle than for a rich man to enter the kingdom of God'. Here 'rich man' isn't an absolute reference, but a reference to men who choose to be rich by hook or by crook. Arjuna sought Krishna and Duryodhana chose Krishna's resources. The rest is history. We all know who triumphed. Let's not trade god for the kingdom of god. If lower ideals can produce such results, then trust me, the higher ideals will only give you a lot more in life. So never go to sleep without answering the third question: 'Day by day, am I living my life in ways by which I am moving closer and closer to my God?' Jai, be worthy of these three questions and life will give you everything else as a natural by-product, and money will be just one of them. Wishing you most and more..."

The 'Best Outgoing Student' of the school was now made ready by Avyakta to be the 'Best Incoming Student' of life.

Money is a wonderful by-product and a very poor point-of-focus. When your work becomes your self-expression, money comes in search of you as a natural by-product. It cannot be the other way around, where money is the point-of-focus and work is only a means to it.

• • •

How you say it, matters!

When struck by an arrow, will you sit around and analyse the raw material with which the arrow is made? When words hurt the tender hearts of people, they care too little for the meaning those words meant to convey. Frankness in itself is never a problem; it is the bluntness with which our frankness is expressed that causes the problem. It isn't just what you cook; how you serve also makes a difference. Good communication will serve a relationship; improper communication will sever a relationship.

Subconscious Doubts and Subconscious Beliefs

A man can be his own take-off pedestal or his own bottleneck. It all depends on how strong his subconscious mind is. Let's learn how to strengthen the subconscious mind.

The appointment was for 3.00 p.m. It was already 3.20 p.m. Siva entered Avyakta's office with a lot of hesitation and uttered a cautious "Sorry!"

Only when mistakes hurt a person, they transform the person. So, there are times when a 'Sorry' from a person should be quietly absorbed. When your response to a 'Sorry' is "It's okay," you are not providing the context for the person to feel the hurt of having committed the mistake. Then, people will only repeat their mistakes.

Avyakta's facial expressions communicated to Siva, "Coming late was not okay." However, the meeting progressed and at the end of the meeting, Siva enquired, "If you are free, can I get something clarified?

This question has been lingering in my head ever since I started relating with you."

"Why do you make such a fuss about punctuality? - Is your question, isn't it?" Avyakta intervened. Siva smiled, nodded his head and waited for Avyakta to reply.

Avyakta shifted from the other side of the table to a chair beside Siva. Avyakta explained, "Siva, existential glory is that all of us are born equals. Human glory lies in ensuring that we do not die as equals. Every human being is made of the same inside stuff and what is possible for one human being is possible for every human being. If all of us are made of the same inside stuff, then, why there is so much disparity in results? One man is able to produce so much, while the rest are not able to? Why is it that for most people, maximum effort produces only minimum results, while for some, minimum effort brings in maximum results? There is a scientific explanation to this."

Curious and connected, Siva waited in eager anticipation for Avyakta to continue. "Listen," said Avyakta, "you said you would meet me at 3.00, but turned up at 3.20. Practically speaking, neither of us is dealing with nanotechnology or rocket science, for 20 minutes to make a difference. However, something beyond the obvious happens. Your 'Sorry' and my acceptance of the same sets everything okay at the conscious level. However, at a much deeper level, your subconscious has made a note of this experience and so has my subconscious. 'When Siva says 3.00, it is not 3.00'. And in your case, this isn't an isolated occurrence, but a repetitive one. Today, in the meeting when you said, 'I will do the project in 15 days', let me be frank with you; internally, I didn't believe you would complete it in 15 days. My conscious mind is able to understand your explanations and the logic behind your projection of 15 days. But my subconscious doesn't trust your commitment. Observations that are recorded from the past reveal that you do not mean what you say. With subtle resistance, it wonders, when 3.00 has never been 3.00, how can I believe 15 will be 15?"

Though cosily sitting in the comfort of an air-conditioned room, there were droplets of sweat forming on Siva's forehead. He wasn't feeling comfortable. He knew he was the subject of Avyakta's narration and that too in an absolute negative connotation.

Avyakta elaborated, "So often have you complained to me that your wife doesn't completely trust your love for her? It is for the same reason. You know you rank the lowest among low, when it comes to your commitment levels. Again, this is not a one-off happening, but a repetitive occurrence in your marriage. At the conscious level, she has no problems with you. But her subconscious does not trust you when you say you love her, because it wonders when 'Tuesdays have never been Tuesdays, 5 has never been 5, tomorrow has never been tomorrow, then how can I believe, when you say love you, it is love you'. The subconscious mind of your wife, even without her being conscious of it, over a period of time, has lost respect for your words. That's why, if you have observed, your son listens to your brother and not to you... ironically, your brother's son listens to you, but not to your brother. Both your brother and you have been consistent defaulters to your own sons, but have been extra good to your nephews. After all, all of us are capable of part-time goodness, but when the same is expected of us full-time, it becomes difficult. By defaulting on promises and commitments to our children, especially when it tends to be repetitive, we lose their subconscious trust. They may not lose respect for us, but they certainly lose respect for our words."

"So Siva, understand," Avyakta continued, "with every faltered commitment, we build a subconscious doubt in the other person. With every promise broken, we develop that subconscious doubt. Since the major portion of the human mind is subconscious and only a small portion of it is the conscious mind, even if everything seems okay at the conscious level, relationships - where subconscious doubts prevail - can never be deep relationships. They remain shallow relationships."

Avyakta added, "The problem is more complicated than you think. Initially, failing commitments and not living up to promises create subconscious doubts in other people and thus affects your relationships. Progressively, your own subconscious develops those doubts and when that happens, it begins to affect your life itself. Every time you aspire to do something big in life, every time you dream of doing something legendary, your own subconscious, because of the doubts you have built due to faltering commitments, will betray your potential. It wonders, 'You can't even wake-up at the time you set the wake-up call', 'You can't even return the call you promised you would', 'You couldn't even deliver the material on the day you promised', 'You can't even make it to an appointment on time'... then, where is the question of you becoming a legend? And, these are not doubts that others have over what you can accomplish, but these are doubts your own subconscious has about you. That's how your own subconscious, because of the prevailing subconscious doubts, betrays your own potential."

Most and more

Siva looked completely shaken up. "Nothing is lost. Everything can be turned around by building subconscious beliefs," consoled Avyakta. "The solution is to understand that with every commitment upheld and every promise fulfilled, it will primarily build subconscious beliefs in you, which will help you to express your potential, and eventually develop subconscious beliefs in others, which will help you to build deep relationships."

"So Siva," Avyakta clarified, "I am not fussy about time; practicing punctuality is one of the tools to develop subconscious beliefs. With such an ordinary background and simple past, if I have reached where I have reached, it is because of the high commitment levels that I practice. Living up to commitments is a wonderful instrument to build subconscious beliefs. It is not about how learned you are or how much knowledge you possess - all these sit in the memory accessible by the conscious mind, but it is about how powerful your subconscious is. With subconscious beliefs, your subconscious works for you. With subconscious doubts, your subconscious works against you. That's why every man is his own take-off pedestal and he is also his own bottleneck."

With a gentle touch on Siva's shoulder Avyakta said, "The greatest pride is to grow in your own eyes.

Every time you live up to your word, you grow in your own eyes and in the process build your subconscious beliefs. The greatest setback is to fall in your own eyes. Every time you are not worthy of your word, you fall in your own eyes and in the process build subconscious doubts. Start with private promises and commitments, and once the commitment muscle is built, you can go public with your promises and commitments."

Avyakta concluded, "Your subconscious must be trained to understand, 'If he says it, he will do it'. Only then it will start believing, 'If he dreams it, he will achieve it'."

Avyakta picked up a piece of paper and wrote on it, "The power of the man is in the power of his mind. The power of his mind is in the power of his subconscious mind. The power of his subconscious mind is in the power of his subconscious beliefs. And, it is these subconscious beliefs that lift man to greatness. All the best Siva! Wishing you most and more..."

Avyakta handed over the note to Siva and Siva replied, "15 days is 15 days. I am on my way to greatness."

The greatest pride is to grow in your own eyes.
The greatest setback is to fall in your own eyes.

Most and more

● ● ●

When you don't give up,
you go up.

Nothing wrong turned out to be right in the long run. The very fact that so many failures have finally turned into success implies that failures are not wrong. So, don't be ashamed of your failures. There is no sunrise without sunset. There is no life without death. There is no success without failures. God's delays are not god's denials. Success delays failures and failures delay success. Failure is a parenthesis inside which success hides and history makers dig them out through relentless striving. If I haven't given up, then I haven't failed. When you don't give up, you go up.

•••

In pushing the lower
the higher delights

Transition is never easy, but without transition there is no evolution. There is no growth within your comfort zone. Unless you are willing to challenge yourself beyond your comfort zones, you cannot become what you can become. Sometimes, you need to give up to go up.

First job, first employer, first boss and first salary... Every 'first' related to your career isn't something you are going to forget in a lifetime. In fact, all career progresses will be benchmarked against these firsts. Your first organisation and your first job can have a major bearing on your work ethics all through your life.

It was a major breakthrough for Sath, Avyakta's son, who had received an offer letter from one of the premium organisations. To many it would have been a dream come true, but Sath was reluctant. He had to relocate himself to a new city and he wasn't prepared to do so. He was very attached to his parents and his friends meant everything to him. Sath argued, "Why should I lose everything I cherish in search of something that is only a promise? I will be happy with any job that doesn't take me away from my friends and my parents."

Avyakta and Sath used to play badminton every morning. While Sath was a natural athlete, Avyakta needed to get into shape. Avyakta's urge to excel in whatever he did and Sath's reckless smashes due to overconfidence balanced the players. The games between them were always competitive. The honours of that morning went to Sath. He won 2-1. Father and son sat in the cafeteria, just outside the badminton court. They had ordered for fresh watermelon juice. Sath was expecting Avyakta to open up, and he wasn't let down.

Avyakta gently wiped the sweat from Sath's forehead with the palm of his right hand and said, "Why sacrifice early morning sleep, why run around the court, why sweat it out? What for? We could have just lazed around in the comfort of our home."

Sath smiled and said, "All that lazing around is the cause of your Indian Standard Tummy (IST)." Saying so, he punched his father's flabby stomach. "Moreover," Sath continued, "how much joy we derive out of being athletic? What fun thumping you 2-1?

How does it feel when the hand-eye coordination is perfect, and to watch the way the feet move? Wow!!! So what, if we have to sweat it out?"

"That's the point Sath," Avyakta retorted. "The law of life is 'When the lower is pushed, the higher delights'. When the body is pushed beyond its perceived limits, the mind delights. When the body tells you 'I can't walk one more block. I can't run another lap. I cannot trek any more', and then when it is pushed beyond its perceived limits and it walks that additional block, runs another lap and treks further - the mind delights. Against the pleading of your body when you do a few more push-ups or a few more reps of the bicep curls or another dozen squats - the mind delights. When the lower - the body is pushed, the higher - the mind delights."

A little on the defensive, Sath enquired, "Well, the concept is wonderful. The philosophy is mind-blowing. But what are you driving at?" By then the juice was served. Father and son exchanged a few uneasy glances through the corner of their eyes. Feeling the fresh, cool juice going down the throat was refreshing.

"You are neither so big that I have to give you an indirect message, nor am I so small that I have to hide my intent and deliver an indirect message to you.

Ours is not a formal relationship, kid. It is a relationship of freedom and openness," Avyakta said and added, "I am going to share something that is life-changing. So listen with devotion. As a continuation to what I have been saying, quietening the mind is a struggle for the mind, but a delight to the intellect. So, whenever you try to do any process to develop your concentration, try to curtail the wandering nature of the mind and get it to focus on a single-point - the mind feels pushed but the higher - the intellect, delights. That's why clarity is always the fruit of concentration."

"Listen, Sath," continued Avyakta, "There is always this inner intellectual conflict between our instincts and conscience. Our instincts ask us to follow the path of 'pain and pleasure' while our conscience demands us to follow the path of 'right and wrong'. It is this that causes the intellectual split in us. What we call as guilt is nothing but the disapproval of the 'knower' in us to an act of the 'doer' in us; that is when the conscience doesn't endorse the instincts. Resolving this split and living as an integrated person is the struggle of the intelligence, but it is the delight of the higher - emotional personality. And so it is at every level. To be caught in the turbulence of various emotions is the natural way of an emotional being. To resolve these emotional turbulences and to be able to live in a state of emotional equanimity is the delight of the higher - the spiritual personality in us. That's why spiritual centeredness is achieved only when man achieves purity in his feelings. With all the examples and explanations, I am trying to drive only one point, 'When the lower is pushed, the higher delights'."

They settled the bill and walked towards the car. Sath took the driver's seat. Avyakta said, "I have never taken decisions for you and I never will. But I can't stop opening up your mind, especially when you are blind to possibilities. If you want an edge over the rest, then you need 'Horizontal Exposure with Vertical Expertise'. Think of anyone you look up to, be it in sports or industry or politics or cinema or even within the family - those who have an edge have it because of 'Horizontal Exposure with Vertical Expertise'. I won't ask you to settle down anywhere other than a place of your choice. I respect your feelings for your parents and friends. In fact, I am proud of you for that. But for sheer exposure, I think you should relocate yourself geographically for some time. So much of your personality will be shaped in the process. I will miss you too. Do you think it is going to be easy for me? But I had made a commitment a long time ago to push my lower self and give that delight to my higher self. "

The car entered the garage. As Sath was about to open the car door, Avyakta said, "Just a minute Sath.

Struggle, suffering, challenges, testing periods, tough times - in fact, all these are part of the vocabulary of a man who is seeing only the lower being pushed without recognising how the higher delights in the process. You are saying the caterpillar is being pushed. I am saying the butterfly is being born. Every time man is pushed, God delights... for, it is through this push that man is created. Align yourself to this spiritual truth and a lot about your life will change."

Sath entered the house, went straight to his room, picked up a book titled 'One Page Wisdom' and went to the restroom. He opened a page at random and read the following story...

At the bottom of a quiet pond lived a little colony of water bugs. They were a happy colony, living far from the sun. They did notice that every once in a while, one from their colony, clinging to a lily stalk gradually moved out of sight and was seen no more. "Look!" said one of the water bugs to others, "One from our colony is climbing up the lily stalk. Where do you think she's going? Wasn't she happy here? Where do you suppose she went?" No one had an answer. Finally one of the water bugs spoke up, "I have an idea. The next one of us to climb up the lily stalk must promise to come back and tell the rest of us where he went and why."

As providence would have it, the very water bug that had suggested the plan found himself climbing up the lily stalk. Up, up and up he went. Before he knew what was happening, he had broken through the surface of the water and fell onto a broad lily pad above. When he opened his eyes, he couldn't believe what he felt. A startling change had come over his old body. His movement revealed four silver wings and a long tail. Even as he struggled, he felt an impulse to move his wings. The warmth of the sun soon dried the moisture from his new body. He moved his wings again and suddenly found himself above the water. He had become a dragonfly.

Swooping and dipping in great curves, he flew through the air. He felt exhilarated in the new atmosphere. He flew happily into his wonderful new world of sun and air. Every now and then, the new dragonfly landed happily on a lily pad to rest. It was then that he chanced to look below, at the bottom of the pond. He was right above his old friends, the water bugs! Then the dragonfly remembered the promise. Without thinking, he dived down. He hit the surface of the water and bounced away. He again landed to rest on the lily pad, of course, having realised:

1. If I had not chosen to outgrow the colony of water bugs, to which I was so attached, I would never have become a dragonfly.

Most and more

2. Now that I have become a dragonfly, even if I want, I can never go back to where I came from.

3. Even if I somehow manage to go back, the colony of water bugs - my old friends - will no longer be able to recognise me in my new form; they won't understand me.

4. I have to wait till one of them also becomes a dragonfly, for, only then will they understand what has happened to me.

Coming out of the restroom, Sath headed towards Avyakta and said, "Dad, till I become you, I won't understand you. However, I have decided to live a life that will delight the Gods. I am ready to be pushed, both horizontally and vertically. Dad, to put it in your words, I am ready for most and more...."

**Struggle, suffering, challenges, testing periods,
tough times - in fact, all these are part of the
vocabulary of a man who is seeing
only the lower being pushed without recognising
how the higher delights in the process.
You are saying the caterpillar is being pushed.
I am saying the butterfly is being born.
Every time man is pushed, God delights...
for, it is through this push that man is created.**

I have the time

The value of 100 rupees is 100 rupees. But the value of one hour depends on who uses that one hour. So, there comes a point in everyone's life, when time becomes your most precious resource.

"It is because of you that your organisation has reached where it has reached. And it is again because of you that your organisation is not becoming what it can become. You were its strength and you have become its weakness. In the long journey of growth, like every other aspect, your strengths too should mature and adapt to changing situations; else, your very strength would become your weakness. Some outstanding graduates struggle to complete their Chartered Accountancy. Why? The methodology of preparation that worked for the graduate course does not work for passing CA. Your approach as a salesman and your approach as a sales manager cannot be the same. As a salesman, your success is your success; but as a sales manager, your team's success is your success. The methodology behind the art of performing is so different from the methodology behind the science of teaching. What worked in building an organisation from 0 to 10 crores will not work if the organisation has to be taken from 10 to 50 crores; and from 500 to 1000 crores is a different story altogether. Your very strength in 'Test' cricket will be your weakness in 'T20'. What you have been has led you up to this point. From here on, unless you change, your future will not change. Your tomorrow will be a mere repetition of your yesterday. If you keep doing the same things, you will keep getting the same results. If you want new results, you have to do new things. You have walked to this point. Now, you will have to trek to the top. The need of the hour is to change yourself as well as your approach," Avyakta boomed.

Though the basis of associations and fraternities seems to be networking, socialising and mutual learning, the fact is that individual egos sometimes feel a little inadequate. Thus, we seek to be in the shadow of a collective ego. Also, collective fear is courage. Associations and fraternities provide that cover for an ego that feels inadequate and insecure. If collectiveness can aid progress, then why not take that path? This evening was part of the fifth anniversary celebrations of the 'Small and Medium Enterprises Association'. Avyakta was invited to be the key speaker of the evening.

He continued his address, "In the beginning of your career and in the infant stages of building an organisation, your most important resource, after yourself, is money. Money influences your decision-making in a big way. You trade your time for money. Then comes a point when time becomes your most precious resource. The value of 100 rupees is 100 rupees. But the value of one hour depends on who uses that one hour. So, there comes a time in your life when you must trade your money for time; in fact, time should become the key factor that influences your decision-making. Will it save me time? Where can I economise time? Is it worth my time? How do I create time for this? Till this point, your criteria for recruitment were to contribute to productivity and profits; but, from now onwards there should also be recruitment to save your time. Keep asking yourself, 'My future comes from where my time goes; so, where should my time go?' Whether it is taking care of your health and fitness, building an organisation, diversifying your business, being there for the family, pursuing your talents and hobbies, reaching out to make a difference to society, or focusing on your spiritual growth - for everything that you want to do, you need to have the time. In essence, we reach a point in life when 'time' almost becomes our God."

Most and more

Most of these men, success stories in their own right, had come to the program with two dominant questions in their mind, "From here, where? From here, how?" Nothing is more gratifying for a teacher than finding a seeker who is ready. While it is true that 'When you are ready, your teacher appears', the converse is not necessarily true. Sometimes, even if the teacher is ready, the student never appears. That's why this group meant a lot to Avyakta. The body language of the participants confirmed their receptivity. It seemed to say, "Show us the path and we will walk it."

Avyakta elaborated, "First-of-all, stop viewing priorities vertically. It is not career first, then family, then health, and so on... Start viewing priorities horizontally. Your career is as important as your family; your health is as important as your spiritual growth, and so on... Several things are equally important in life. In an organisation, the efficiency of the accounts department is as significant as the maintenance; sales is as important as costing; purchase is as important as servicing; so on and so forth. The question is not 'Out of everything, which is the best' but 'How to get the best out of everything?' Nothing can happen at the cost of something else. Then the question is, 'How can we achieve this with 24-hours being a constant'?"

Typical of any audience, there were people of all kinds. There were those who noted everything using technology, also those who relied on the good old method of paper and pen, and of course those who followed the most traditional and proven method of learning - listening intently and getting instantly transformed. It is so important that you commit what you learn to your intelligence, and act on it; and not let it remain as a piece of mere unapplied knowledge in memory, paper and technology.

"Apply the formula of 'Top-5' to anything and everything in your life," said Avyakta. "Identify your Top-5 customers and interact with them at a personal level. Give them your time and attention. Not a week should go by without your interacting with the Top-5 in some way. That on which you invest time grows. Either you invest time on your Top-5 customers or your competition will. Haven't you gone through this? Sometimes when your key employee resigns, he also walks away with some of your most important customers. When you lose some of your customers from the bottom of your clientele, it doesn't affect the organisation that much. But when you lose even a couple from the top of your clientele, it can have a tremendous bearing on the business. So, find your Top-5 customers and systematise your investment of time with them."

Most and more

To an audience that was opening up with every passing moment, Avyakta continued, "Similarly, work with your Top-5 employees. It is unfortunate that in most organisations the trouble-making employees get more attention than the employees who are most productive. When you lose one of your top employees, you lose a trained resource. It not only weakens your organisation, but also strengthens the competition. The basis of loyalty is relationship, and relationships cannot be built without an investment of time. Not a week should go by without your interacting with the Top-5 in some way. The formula of Top-5 extends to everything - suppliers, stocks, inflows, outflows, friends, roles, etc... In every dimension of your life, identify the Top-5 and systematise your investment of time on them. The formula of Top-5 will ensure that things that matter the most in your life are not at the mercy of things that matter the least in life. What's important to you will now get your time. And to get your time, it has to become important to you."

Avyakta further added, "Build your whole organisation on this model. Ask your next in line to focus on the Next-5, and the third in line on the 5 after that... Also understand, because your Top-5 will keep changing as you keep growing, some of your current Top-5 in certain categories will become part of the Next-5 of your next in line, and some of his will move into the 5 of the third line - forming an efficient time-pyramid."

Avyakta concluded, "With the formula of Top-5, your time will go where it should go, and nowhere else. Take care of your time and you have taken care of one of the Gods of your life. I wish that one of you grow to become one in my Top-5. I wish I could mentor one of you personally. Start from where you can start. So, first identify the Top-5 areas in which you want to implement the formula of Top-5."

And with a genuine intent resonating in his voice that people should make it to the top, Avyakta said, "Thank you so much. I am glad I had the time to come here this evening. And for my Top-5, I will always have the time. All the best! Wishing you most and more..."

Avyakta walked. And the rest, were ready to trek to the top.

Keep asking yourself,
'My future comes from where my time goes;
so, where should my time go?'
For everything that you want to do,
you need to have the time.
In essence, we reach a point in life
when 'time' almost becomes our God.

●●●

To live is to live fearlessly

To live is to live fearlessly. Nothing stops
man as fear does. Fear stops man from the
possibilities of greatness more than any
other single factor. Fear must be
overcome. Understand the mechanism of
fear. It is not because you fear you avoid
things, but it is because you avoid things it
becomes fear. That which you do not face
controls you; that which controls you
causes fear in you. Do the very thing you
fear. Expect to be afraid, but still do it.
Face fear fearlessly. Repeatedly face what
you fear and fear will be vanquished.

●●●

Whose life are you living?

History makers are those who choose to rewrite the script of their lives. Revolution is all about rewriting the script. To break through, you need to break with. The real voyage of discovery consists not in seeking new landscapes, but in having new eyes.

"Who knows what lies ahead? The joys and sorrows, the opportunities and challenges, laughter or tears of the coming day, who knows what lies ahead? Who cares about what lies ahead? The moment of truth is that you are alone in the bathroom and in the here and now in the bathroom, you reign. The moment has come to embark upon a grand adventure into the unknown. It is time to brush your teeth! You have two choices. You can go about it the same way you have; repeat a few mechanical motions. The other is to experiment. Start the day on a new tone. Face the mirror and roar like a lion. Roar as loudly as your surroundings permit. The roar will immediately bring energy into the body and bring your body to the present moment. It will awaken the slumbering beast within. You are permitted to laugh if you find it funny.

Most and more

Usually we take ourselves too seriously, and a good laugh at nothing in particular, miraculously puts things back into perspective. So laugh. Feel at home in your body. Be yourself. It is your bathroom; you are alone, you reign in the here and now, and this perhaps is a rare opportunity."

Dressed in formals, with tablet computers in front of them, seated in a U-formation in the conference room, they looked at one another. It was a group of fresh business management graduates, twenty in number, supposedly, in an induction program. It was going to be a three-day orientation program and the last segment of each day was an address by their Chief Mentor, Avyakta. Their minds were barely prepared to listen to a speech on what to do first thing in the morning in the bathroom! Everyone's body language expressed disbelief.

Avyakta continued. "At first, these small exercises may appear childish; as a matter of fact, they are. But in pursuit of flashier jobs and higher incomes, we've lost our ability to look within and are no more able to connect with our own selves. Often our fast pace makes us forget what we are running after. Learn to play again. Rediscover the childlike delight in simple things. It will help stimulate your creative side and make your imagination run wild. Children don't put down their ideas; instead, they jump with wild enthusiasm, excited by their originality. Let go of your conditioned adult mind. Coming back to your teeth, brushing need not be a grind. Slip the brush into all the small spaces and crevices. Be sensual, be imaginative and don't be shy. Experiment with different speeds, rhythms and movements. Use your non-natural hand for brushing. Brushing with the other hand is an exciting experience because you have to learn it anew; the unpractised hand cannot do it automatically. The best way to learn is to consciously brush with your natural hand and then imitate the movement with the learning hand. Several interesting things will happen in the process. The teaching hand learns to be more relaxed and probably becomes more efficient. The learning hand picks up a new skill. Furthermore, the brain is stimulated in a new way and called upon to function beyond its usual limit."

Smiling at the frozen faces, Avyakta concluded, "Gentlemen, this assignment is a very important part of your induction, and it is mandatory. Go through the experience and submit a report on the experience tomorrow."

Though the assignment seemed weird, Avyakta had certainly kindled their curiosity and inquisitiveness. They subjected themselves to the experiences and also presented their reports. They had never thought that 'brushing of teeth' would be a major point of discussion in an induction program for handpicked business management graduates. It was a choiceless situation for these management trainees. Ironically, Avyakta didn't even go through their reports. Instead they were given another assignment that would make the fathers of management studies turn in their graves. Each one of them were given the latest annual report of the organisation and asked to submit a proposal on how to lead the company to closure within three years. "Guys and girls, in three years time we should be out of business. I know the focus of all your learning has been on how to build a business. It is time to challenge your thinking in a new direction. The crux of creativity is seeing things from a new perspective. The greatest block to creativity is old judgements. It is time to reprogram your minds. Try the untried," exclaimed Avyakta.

Most of them didn't even blink their eyes that night. They thought individually; they brainstormed collectively; they surfed the Net. The night was long and the morning came rather early. This was their first glimpse of corporate India. 'Pressure' - that's the oxygen of the new corporate world. That's what they breathe and that's what they live on. It seems 'Sssstttttrrrrreeettttttcccccchhhhhhh' is the only way.

In the concluding session, the last and final one before they would take on their responsibilities thus spoke Avyakta: "I am not trying to give you a new management paradigm; we actually need a new social paradigm. From the time we are born, we learn to live within boundaries and parameters. We are conditioned by our physical environment, by what our parents and others tell us, by events that impact us emotionally, and by the subtle social structures that surround us. We are all 'bred' to play our roles. Of course, conditioning allows us to live together and work together. But, slowly and relentlessly, we build a 'box' around ourselves. Adults quickly become comfortable inside their individual boxes and continue to live on 'autopilot'. We tend to see only what we already know. As a species, we seem to look for ways to maintain the status quo. We get settled into old habits. We learn to adapt to their constrictions and therefore forget that there are boundaries. How many times have we humans found ourselves repeating the same old patterns, hoping for better results? A responsible person must learn to unlearn what he has learned. A responsible person must have the courage to rethink and change his thoughts. Are you willing to unlearn and relearn? Are we willing to play a different game? We are simply living a social script that has been handed over to us. It is your life, but someone else's script - the script handed down by parents, the society and the community. Whose life are you living? How do we escape from the box?"

Even at the thought level, no one seemed to be contradicting what Avyakta was saying. The silence in the hall and the rapt attention with which everyone was listening was a confirmation of that. Avyakta continued. "Thinking about one's thinking lays the foundation for 'learning to unlearn'. By allowing ourselves to be different, we give ourselves permission to be excellent, instead of being ordinary. Just as we cannot plant new crops without first pulling out the old roots and giving the new seeds a chance, we need to unlearn before we can learn anew. Unlearning is the key. Learning is more than the mere acquisition of new knowledge and insights; it is also crucial to unlearn old knowledge that has outlived its relevance. Thus, forgetting the old is probably as important as remembering the new. To generate new ideas, you have to accelerate the unlearning of old ones. The most important lessons lie not in what you need to learn, but in what you need to unlearn. Your old strengths in a new environment become your new weaknesses. Sometimes, we need to go down a few grades to learn something new. Sometimes, you have to step back in order to step forward, and in it you will feel the renewed energy. The power in the unlearning process is found in its ability to challenge and destroy some of the concepts that we hold dear. We need to revisit old beliefs with new minds."

"Gentlemen, listen!" Avyakta roared. "I am not seeing you as architects of the future of this organisation alone, but as the torch bearers of a new world. Pathfinders have to be path-breakers. Develop a conscious desire to explore possibilities outside your conditioned thinking. It might make you aware of what lies outside the box, and perhaps help you see and hear things that you were previously oblivious to. You will gradually develop a creative tension between your desire to change and your resistance, which is a fear of the unknown. You could challenge the old model, unlearn that which was holding you back, and begin to open up enough to destroy the old box and create anew. When this happens, it will be a moment of breakthrough and great awareness. Such transformations lead to dramatic increase in openness and create a space, a gap, between present reality and the future vision."

Avyakta ended by saying, "History makers are those who choose to rewrite the script of their lives. Revolution is all about rewriting the script. To break through, you need to break with. The real voyage of discovery consists not in seeking new landscapes, but in having new eyes. See you in the future that do not resemble our past. Thank you. Love you. Wishing you most and more…"

The management graduates experientially realised: What one can learn from a man, one cannot learn from books. Encyclopaedia is one thing. A living encyclopaedia is completely another. In Avyakta, they found a living encyclopaedia.

Nothing like growing in the right hands.

Pathfinders have to be path-breakers.
Develop a conscious desire to explore possibilities
outside your conditioned thinking. It might make
you aware of what lies outside the box,
and perhaps help you see and hear things that
you were previously oblivious to.
You will gradually develop a creative tension
between your desire to change and your
resistance, which is a fear of the unknown.
You could challenge the old model, unlearn that
which was holding you back, and begin to open
up enough to destroy the old box and create anew.
When this happens, it will be a moment of
breakthrough and great awareness.

My Success & I

Many people have failed because they could not handle their success. Many celebrities have succumbed to various forms of intoxication because they were unable to handle the magnitude of their success. Few fall to rise. Many rise to fall. How do we handle success?

"I knew from the beginning that those chickens wouldn't make it. Honestly, I didn't think I had a competitor. In fact, I wonder how our 'chief' manages these bananas. Everything has to be repeated to them several times. Their grasp is so pathetic. You've got to have some brains... I think they should eat more walnuts and almonds. What do you say?" Amidst laughter and giggles, this was the conversation between Avyakta's daughter and her friend. The awards ceremony had taken place today and Dolly received the 'Best Employee of the Year' award. Her friend had called Dolly to congratulate her and this was a portion of the conversation between them.

Avyakta was reclining in a traditional 'easy chair' in the balcony of his house. Two parrots had stopped over on the *neem* tree, which the balcony overlooked.

Avyakta had been listening to the parrots' chatter till his daughter's tone on the phone caught his attention. For a man who always believed that a true champion not only wins the award but also the hearts of those who didn't make it, this tone from his daughter was a shocker.

'What you become' means nothing if it comes at the cost of 'Who you are'. There are good people and there are successful people. But great are those who remain good even after becoming successful. Avyakta, like most fathers, had unreasonably high expectations from his daughter. He wanted her to be good, successful and also great. What are relationships for, if you can't even tell a person he is wrong when you feel he is wrong? There can be no depth in a relationship where there is a compulsive need to please the other every time, all the time. Such relationships will only be too superficial and shallow. You don't derive fulfilment out of these relationships. The depth of a relationship is revealed by the freedom and openness that's possible in communication in that relationship. Open communication helps you to either clarify or get clarified.

Avyakta knew that he could take this freedom with Dolly. Metaphorically, relationships are like bank accounts - emotional accounts. You can withdraw from the relationship only to the extent you have deposited in the relationship. If I have done enough in the relationship, then I can take enough from the relationship. Some accounts are over-deposited. In such relationships, even a major issue is handled as a trifle. Some accounts are overdrawn. In those relationships, even trifle issues are major. For a man who always believed in going into a relationship looking at what he can give and not at what he can receive, most of Avyakta's relationships were over-deposited. This gave him great freedom in most of his relationships. And out of this freedom, he called Dolly, "Sweetheart, if I can have a few minutes with you..."

The lovely daughter, instead of proceeding towards the balcony, walked towards the kitchen. Avyakta's focus shifted back to the *neem* tree, but the parrots were not there. The green against the blue background looked celestial. Here and there were a few strokes of white and grey. It was an unusually sultry morning. There was no breeze and the leaves were in a state of meditative stillness. "Your *masala chai* is ready!" the voice came first and then came Dolly. One weakness Avyakta had chosen to live with was his weakness for tea. He couldn't refuse good *chai*. And Dolly, she always pressed the right buttons. It is not without reason that she was chosen the 'Best Employee'.

Most and more

"Hmmm..." sipping the steaming cup of tea, Avyakta said, "Dolly, I know these are very special moments of celebration for you. Your heart must be dancing. Nothing tastes like success." Dolly, who was sitting on the floor, rested her hands on Avyakta's lap, gently leaned forward and planted a kiss on his stomach. "Thank you pa..." she said.

Placing the tea cup back on the garden bench, Avyakta continued, "Truth be told... I didn't like the tone in which you spoke on the phone. Chickens, bananas, got to have brains - what sort of words and phrases to describe people? Just because you have tasted one major success, hmmm?"

Dolly withdrew her hands from Avyakta's lap and became a little formal. She moved a few feet away from her father. With her back resting against the wall, she sat in a place from where she could look into her father's eyes. Avyakta could do anything, say anything, and Dolly would not misunderstand him. To her, her father was not just a relationship. He was her faith. "Tell me pa..."

Avyakta spoke, "Do you know how many people have failed because they could not handle their success? Do you know how many celebrities have succumbed to various forms of intoxication because they could not handle the magnitude of their success? Few fall to rise.

Many rise to fall. Let success not make my sweetheart into a bitter-heart. The higher you go, if you fall, the deeper the fall will be. Beware, my child."

Tears welled up in Dolly's eyes. "Did I disappoint you pa?"

"Just because I am correcting you, it does not mean that you let me down. Feedbacks don't mean you are not good. I know it is typical to assume, 'they think I am not good enough and that's why they are giving me a feedback'. But, if good can become great, then why not? Dolly, I have always shared the ingredients of success with you. Now that you are beginning to taste success, I think I have the responsibility to coach you on the way to handle success," clarified Avyakta.

The invitation of love and affection that was flowing through Avyakta's eyes drew Dolly close to him once again. Her hands were once again on Avyakta's lap. A pinch on her cheeks, a pat on her head, and Avyakta continued, "Success should never feed your ego, but must always feed your sense of responsibility. Success is not a status. It is a responsibility. Your next promotion is not a status. It only means are responsible for the success of a lot more people in your team. Being made the captain of an Indian cricket team only means that you are now responsible for the aspirations and sentiments of a billion people.

Becoming the Prime Minister only means that you are now responsible for the future of a nation. Being elected as the President of a social organisation only means that it is your responsibility to ensure that the resources at your disposal will serve the right social needs during your tenure. With every rung you scale on the ladder of success, you are also scaling rungs on the ladder of responsibility. Aspiring to be successful, in essence, is aspiring to be more responsible."

Avyakta further added, "Dolly, also understand that every man is a product of a huge investment. From God, to parents, to teachers, to society, to mentors, to colleagues, to all men who left a trail behind for us to follow, to people whose names and forms we may never know - everybody plays a part in the making of every man. Nobody makes it alone. In truth, nobody is self-made. All of us are made by others. The success we produce is just our way of justifying the investments that have been made on us. We are mere instruments of success. Success, per se, is a collective force. It just culminates through a few individuals and this time it happened to be you. I am not taking away any credit from you for what you have achieved. After all, not every bamboo becomes a flute in the hands of a Master. You have to be a bamboo worthy of a Master. You have to be the one that's worthy of being the instrument of success. But success can never burden those who see themselves as an instrument. See yourself as an instrument and your life will be all music. Hey little one, in every way, you deserve most and more..."

"*Appa*," Dolly intervened, "Thank you. From here on, success will only make me more and more responsible to lift not only myself but others as well. To me, success will also mean that I should progressively become a worthy instrument of the collective force called 'success' and eventually, one day, I should become His instrument in the lives of my fellow humans."

The parrots were back on the *neem* tree, and they were talking. Between Dolly and Avyakta, there had been enough talking. It was now time to walk the talk...

Success should never feed your ego, but must always feed your sense of responsibility. Success is not a status. It is a responsibility. With every rung you scale on the ladder of success, you are also scaling rungs on the ladder of responsibility. Aspiring to be successful, in essence, is aspiring to be more responsible.

● ● ●

Activity Vs Productivity

Let us not mistake activity for
productivity. Time and effort can
never be managed in isolation.
They are always managed in
the context of what you want
from life and where you want to
reach in life. Effort without
direction is activity. Effort with
direction is productivity.

• • •

Progressive Maturity

Growth and time are inseparable. With efficient methodologies, time factor can be shrunk, but never eliminated. Child to adulthood, whether physical or emotional or psychological, needs time. Mental development needs time. Maturity needs time. Personalities or organisations or civilisation grow with time. Attempting to cram the whole process, searching for short cuts to development and trying quick-fix solutions may provide instant gratifications, but never long-term results. There are no ambitious goals, only ambitious time frames. Maturity and transformation are, and can only be, progressive phenomena.

The economy was booming and this retail chain was experiencing explosive growth. As it happens with every growing organisation, there were leadership and manpower crisis. None of the 3 Ms - Market, Money and Machinery - were an issue; they were available in abundance. The issue was with the 4th M - Manpower. Competent manpower becoming scarce was an industry crisis. The only option left was to recruit and train freshers to the required level of competence. Instead of recruiting people on the merit of their experience and past performance, the organisation decided to recruit people for the promise they showed. The focus shifted from the expired past to an expected future. Fresh minds, in hundreds, joined the payroll. And to train them, Rajesh, the Chairman of the retail chain, approached his mentor Avyakta.

It is always better to begin with the end in mind. When objectives are defined, then the processes to achieve the objectives can be defined. For understanding to happen, words must have the same meaning to the listener as well as the communicator. So, Avyakta had an elaborate discussion with Rajesh, instead of making assumptions. Rajesh was restless. He wanted instant results. How can you expect today's results by yesterday, when the very process is going to begin only tomorrow? Rajesh was aware that Avyakta had the practice of designing all his training schedules over a prolonged period of time. Rajesh didn't have the time to wait. Though extremely restless within, out of sheer respect for Avyakta, Rajesh requested with humility, "Please don't slow me down. I want you to come up with some quick solutions - a one-day seminar, a two-day workshop, whatever - but I want immediate results. Please... we don't have the time for all those long-drawn programs."

Avyakta smiled and then added, "You know I don't do those overnight *buddhu* to Buddha programs. If you want to throw money on the street, do so. But don't get me involved in all this. I understand your passion, and I can empathise with your restlessness. We are not talking about mending toys here, but about mentoring minds. Developing a mind takes time. Cultivation is a process that involves various stages - preparing the soil, sowing the seeds, removing the weeds, nourishing it with manure and water, protecting it and waiting for the entire duration of the growth cycle of the crop... until it is ready for harvesting. There is no way to cram this process. There are no short cuts in the laws of nature. Nature does not allow cramming. You go against natural laws at your own peril. Haven't we blundered in school and college? We studied for our exams only at the eleventh hour. As a result, we passed the exams, got the degrees, but deprived ourselves of the knowledge. We did become graduates in maths and graduates in chemistry, but we don't remember anything about the subject. A quick-fix program will pass on a lot of information, but will not create any transformation. You will have the false satisfaction of having trained your people and my bank account will have undeserving money (money that causes dissatisfaction to those who gave it is undeserving money; it never serves a good purpose)."

Most and more

Rajesh's head dropped and his shoulders drooped. "Now what?" his eyes pleaded for a solution.

Avyakta gently patted Rajesh and said, "I understand you. But I also want you to understand me. Growth and time are inseparable. With efficient methods, the time factor can be shrunk, but never eliminated. Childhood to adulthood, whether physical or emotional or psychological, needs time. Mental development needs time. Maturity needs time. Growth needs time, whether it pertains to individuals, organisations or civilisations. Attempting to cram the whole process, seeking short cuts to development and trying quick-fix solutions may provide instant gratification, but never long-term results. There are no ambitious goals, only ambitious time frames. Every development has a timescale - the earth takes 24 hours to rotate on its own axis and 365.25 days to revolve around the sun. This timescale cannot be altered. It takes x-months for the newborn to develop speech and n-months for him to walk. Time is an ingrained ingredient of development. Natural laws are not alterable. They are not subject to human re-engineering. Simply put, there is no elevator to the top. You've got to take the steps."

Rajesh's body language suggested a reluctant 'Okay, let us have it your way.'

Avyakta said, "This story will illustrate my point."

An innocent villager came to a city. Starving, he stopped at a roadside eatery and asked the waiter, "What can you give me that will satiate my hunger?" "Vada is good," was the reply. "What will be the cost of the vada that will satisfy my hunger?" asked the hungry man. "Five rupees," was the prompt reply. The villager enquired, "Are you telling me that vada will satisfy my hunger and it will cost me five rupees?" Now a little irritated, the waiter asked in return, "Do you want the vada or not?" The man ordered for the vada, consumed the first and he was still hungry. So he went for the second, but it didn't appease his hunger. Then went in the third, fourth, fifth, even the sixth - his stomach seemed to be a bottomless pit. He was still hungry. Finally, the seventh vada worked. His hunger was satiated. The innocent man took out a five-rupee coin and handed it to the waiter. To his utter shock, the waiter demanded thirty-five rupees, and clarified, "You had seven vadas." The villager shot back, "I clearly asked you, 'What is the cost of the vada that will satisfy my hunger?' and you said 'five rupees'. Only the seventh satisfied my hunger; the other six did not achieve the purpose. So I will pay only for the seventh, not for the remaining six."

"See, if the seventh vada was not preceded by the six, it couldn't have made the difference. If only six vadas had gone in, it wouldn't still have made the difference. The Zen expression says 'When you are ready your teacher will appear'; it is basically referring to those six *vadas*, which make you ready, and the seventh *vada* is the transformation. Even with the Zen concept of '*Satori*', which is supposedly instant awakening, there is a process of developing the mind to a state where the mind becomes capable of experiencing '*Satori*'. Even effortlessness is achieved only through effort."

Avyakta further elaborated, "Rajesh, maturity is a progressive phenomenon. Even when it is instant, the reality is that the mind has actually progressed to the point where this instant transformation is possible. Man cannot escape the four stages of progressive maturity. He is so designed. The four stages are:

Firstly, Unconscious Incompetence: *I don't know that I don't know.* This is the stage of blissful ignorance before learning begins. As a child I thought that all I needed to do was to sit behind the wheel and steer, and the car would go. Similarly in public speaking, I had the mannerism of saying 'um' frequently, but was not aware of it.

Secondly, Conscious Incompetence: *I know that I don't yet know how to do it.* This is where learning begins. Then I realised that there was a whole lot more to driving a car, and I felt a little daunted. However,

103

someone pointed out to me that I use 'um' extensively as space filler in public speaking.

Thirdly, Conscious Competence: *I know that I know how to do this.* This stage is uncomfortable because you are self-conscious. As I practiced driving I felt a lot better. My driving was still a little jerky. I often had to think about what to do next, and that felt awkward and uncomfortable. Once consciously aware of the issue, I began to make an effort to overcome the mannerism of 'um' in my speaking. Effort and conscious attention were still required.

Finally, Unconscious Competence: *What I do, I do well.* The final stage when the capability has become a natural part of us. We don't have to think about it. Finally, after enough practice, I got to the place where I didn't have to think about every little thing I was doing while driving. Eventually however, the behaviour of consciously avoiding saying 'um' and replacing it with silent pauses becomes habitual, internalised and automatic. Today, I don't even have to think to excel at public speaking."

"Also remember Rajesh," Avyakta concluded, "Incompetence is born out of three factors. They are lack of information, lack of understanding and lack of experience. Only through listening can the first lack be removed, which will be my programs.

Most and more

Self-contemplation alone will remove the second lack, which is why we need time between sessions. Only through implementation will the third lack be removed, which is why I always have a long span for the program."

Rajesh acknowledged, "The ways of a teacher a teacher alone understands. Today I have realised, I can define the results I seek; but the expert has to define the process and the time frame for the results."

Avyakta concluded, "As much as I say that there are no overnight *buddhu* to Buddha, I am also convinced that every one of us can progressively mature from a *buddhu* to a Buddha. Man is designed for most and more... to experience abundance in every form."

Incompetence is born out of three factors.
They are lack of information,
lack of understanding and lack of experience.
Only through listening can the first lack be
removed. Self-contemplation alone will remove
the second lack. Only through implementation
will the third lack be removed.
As much as there are no overnight *buddhu* to
Buddha, yet, every one of us can progressively
mature from a *buddhu* to a Buddha.

Who is the Master?

Either you run your life, or your habits run your life. Who is the Master and who is the slave? Let's get our perceptions right.

'From here, where?' was the topic of the seminar. The key speakers in the seminar were Dev and Avyakta. Dev was a path-breaking management coach and Avyakta, a pathfinder in social reforms. Together they were addressing the 'movers and shakers' of the country on, 'From here, where?'

Dev and Avyakta were both orators par excellence. They could make even a dead man turn in his grave. Whatever they spoke, the questions they answered, the discussions they facilitated were reforming and transforming. Strangely, Dev was getting a little ego involved with Avyakta. By the end of the seminar, Dev spared no opportunity to counter and negate some of Avyakta's answers. For the seminar participants it was a pure intellectual delight to see two legendary thinkers at loggerheads.

After the seminar, people were fraternising during dinnertime. And the modern-day-unavoidable - cocktails, were being served. Avyakta, a strict teetotaller, had a crowd gathered around him. Dev, a strict liquid spiritualist, too had a crowd around him. The spirit of alcohol fuelled Dev's ego even more. With a glass of scotch in one hand and a cigarette in the other, Dev walked towards Avyakta, as if he had some scores to settle. Out of sheer respect for the legendary Dev, the crowd moved to the side, as if they had cordoned off a pathway. Avyakta greeted Dev with a smile and added, "They seem to have gained a lot from your insights. That's what they were sharing with me. They were saying that some of your thoughts are path-breaking."

"Thank you Avyakta," acknowledged Dev and added, "I have heard you saying 'In matters of principle, stand like a rock and in matters of relationship, flow like the river'. For the sake of relationship, why don't you join us for a drink?"

Avyakta burst out laughing and then said, "That's innovative, asking me to drink in the name of relationship. I always thought 'to drink or not' was a matter of principle. Anyways Dev, you have your ways. You want me to drink with you, right? How does it matter to you what is in the glass and what goes down my throat, as long as I stand next to you sipping a glass?" Saying so, Avyakta picked up a glass of fruit punch.

'I and I alone will have the last say' is one of the most common traits of an egoist. Dev was not going to lie low and take this. Dev argued, "Why is it that you people who abstain from some habits think very high of yourselves? And what is so bad about those of us who enjoy the little pleasures of life? Even some doctors, who understand everything about the way the body functions, drink. Then what's all this fuss about?"

Avyakta explained, "Alcohol is just incidental. The fuss is not about alcohol, but about habits. I am not saying there are good habits and bad habits. Habits, whether they pertain to liquor or tea or TV or newspaper, are wrong." Avyakta took a sip of the fruit punch and said, "If I didn't get this fruit punch today it wouldn't have mattered to me, but if you didn't get what's in your glass it would have disturbed you. Habits disturb one's flow and happiness. Hence they are wrong."

Dev snubbed him saying, "Typical people, all of you. What you do is right and what you don't do is wrong. If we are like you, we are good people; if not, we are bad people." Saying so Dev walked out of the place, of course with the satisfaction that he had the last say. It was more than certain that Dev would never share a platform again with Avyakta.

Most and more

One of the seminar organisers who had been instrumental in bringing Dev to the seminar extended a soft apology to Avyakta. Avyakta said, "When you hold your peace above everything else, then no thing and no one can disturb you. When you hold your ego above everything else, then every thing and every one disturbs you. For me, it is first my peace, and then everything else. I have come a long way in this path and the Dev(s) don't control my peace anymore."

One of the seminar participants stepped forward and enquired, "With all due respect and no offence meant to you, I am truly curious to know what is wrong with habits. What do you mean when you say that there are no good or bad habits, but that all habits are wrong?"

Avyakta explained, "Habits are mental phonograph records. Repeated indulgence in anything creates a mental blueprint. Whenever one puts the needle of attention on the grooves formed in the mind, it plays back the blueprint. Repetition causes the grooves to deepen and after a while, the record plays automatically, over and over again. The mental make-up, the patterns called habit become hard set, making it difficult to change. Thus we become slaves to our habits and lose our freedom, self-discipline and control. Our habits make us lead a robot-like existence."

Avyakta elaborated, "Haven't we heard about the Pavlov effect? Ivan Pavlov used to ring a metronome at the same time he fed his dogs. After a while, the dogs that earlier salivated only on seeing their food, began to salivate when the metronome sounded, even if no food was present. Can man suffer like Pavlov's dogs? But that's what habits are. If I don't smoke, I can't do potty; without something to read, I can't sit on the pot; if I miss my morning tea, I will get a headache; if I don't have a banana in the night, I won't be able to sleep; when I am tense, I need a drink; no matter what happens I will run home to watch my favourite mega serial, else hell will break lose... ring the bell and I will salivate. Salvation or Salivation?!"

"To be succinct," Avyakta said, "If you do not get what you want when you want it, and it disturbs you, it has gained mastery over you. What has gained mastery over you has gained mastery over your peace. The more external masters you have, the less peaceful you are. If the newspaper is delayed, it disturbs your peace. If the coffee is not to your specification, it disturbs your peace. If you can't go to the temple when you want to, it disturbs your peace. Even going to places of worship has become a conditioned mechanical response - a habit. If going or not going to the temple disturbs your peace, then even your relationship with the force above has become habitual.

That which does not give you peace and that which disturbs your peace, how can it be spirituality?"

"Dev should have stayed here," commented one of the participants. "That's right," acknowledged a few others.

Avyakta clarified, "The proof of right living is in the peace that you experience. Habits disturb your peace and hence all habits are wrong. Will Power is developed through 'Won't Power'. The next time you don't get something when you want it, and it disturbs you, understand it has gained mastery over you. Practice 'Won't Power'. For one full week abstain from that which disturbed you. Again get back to it. But if not getting it when you want it continues to disturb you, practice 'Won't Power' again for another week... till you either gain complete mastery over it or no more need it, forever. Take it one week at a time and achieve a triumph of a lifetime."

Avyakta summarised, "Who is the Master is the big question? The more number of times the answer is something or someone outside of you, then you do not have a very peaceful existence. The more number of times you feel you are the Master, you will find that you are experiencing the all-encompassing peace."

Avyakta concluded, "Everything that comes into our life should either stay with us and become our strength, or it should leave us and make us free. It should never stay with us and become our weakness. Even Avyakta, experience him as a choice and not as an addiction. Allow me to be your strength and not a weakness."

The Master left asking others to become the master.

If you do not get what you want when you want it, and it disturbs you, it has gained mastery over you. What has gained mastery over you has gained mastery over your peace.
The more external masters you have, the less peaceful you are. The proof of right living is in the peace that you experience.
Habits disturb your peace and hence all habits are wrong.
Will Power is developed through 'Won't Power'. Practice 'Won't Power'. For one full week abstain from that which disturbed you.
Again get back to it. But if not getting it when you want it continues to disturb you, practice 'Won't Power' again for another week… till you either gain complete mastery over it or no more need it, forever. Take it one week at a time and achieve a triumph of a lifetime.

Most and more

●●●

Evolving Consciousness

We are all given life, to add something
to life. When 'a' man lives his life with
heightened awareness, his life helps
humanity to gain a few years of maturity
without they having to live those few
years. In effect, 'he' fast forwards
humanity by a few years. Every being,
who is living his life with heightened
awareness, is actually doing God's work...
he has been delegated a responsibility
by Existence to play a part in evolving
human consciousness.

●●●

Oh! Not again...

If you feel it is a repetition then you are not growing through that experience. Only when you stagnate, you start viewing experiences as repetition.

Yajus was completely engrossed in his *pranayama*. The discipline of rising before sunrise and committing 90 minutes to Yoga has been a part of Yajus's life for three years now. Yajus was not at peace with himself today. His mind was far more chaotic than it normally is. One of the expressions of human intelligence is asking questions. Questions can lead you to clarity; questions can also lead you to chaos. "How long should I be practicing the same method of *pranayama*?" was the question that had risen in Yajus's mind!

The mind needs variety. It thrives on new circus. For example, eating the same type of food is good for the body. The body learns to handle it. The inner constitution gets tuned to it. But the mind feels a sense of monotony when you eat the same kind of food. It needs variation. So we indulge in different types of food to satiate the impulses of the mind and fall sick as a result. Waking up at the same time, eating at a fixed time and going to bed at the same time helps the body to tune its biorhythms for a healthy lifestyle. A time for everything and everything in its time - that's what discipline is all about and it absolutely suits the body. But the mind feels suffocated by such monotony. "What is the point if today is just a repetition of yesterday?" the mind wonders. So the mind pulls you into indisciplined indulgence.

In fact, the very desire of the mind to get away from monotony draws us towards various forms of intoxication. Intoxication confuses the mind by depressing the central nervous system (CNS). Under normal circumstances the central nervous system receives sensory information from the organs, analyses it, and then initiates an appropriate response. However, when one is intoxicated, the alcohol or nicotine interferes with the central nervous system's ability to analyse sensory information. This results in the typical symptoms of impaired judgement, inappropriate behaviour, diminished response of the senses, slowed mental processing, intensified emotions and lowered inhibitions. However, because there is variety in this internal drama and the mind finds it entertaining, the mind gets us to indulge in various forms of intoxication.

That's why a person can never be brought out of any addiction without rehabilitating the mind.

Yajus's mind was playing with him, "How long should I be practicing the same method of *pranayama*?" Once a question is born, unless answered and resolved, it continues to cause agitation. It is called Arjuna's predicament. You cannot be good at even that, which you are good at, unless the questions are resolved. Avyakta is both, Yajus's father as well guru. So Yajus approached Avyakta. The body never lies. From Yajus's facial expressions, Avyakta knew that the boy was not at peace with himself.

"When you initiated me into this *pranayama* you told me to practice it continuously for 21 days," Yajus said. "I have been repeating the same for three years now. It's getting a little boring - the same stuff, the same thing repeated day after day. If you were just my father, it would have been easy for me to express my irritation; but you are also my guru. And hence I was holding it back; but I can't take it anymore."

"If you feel it is a repetition," Avyakta said, "then you are not growing through that experience. Only when you stagnate, you start viewing experiences as repetition. In growth there are no repetitions, though it appears to be the same on the surface."

Most and more

"I know you will say it is 'typical' of me, yet I want to tell you a story," Avyakta said. "A long time ago in China, there were monasteries where monks lived, grew their own food, made their own clothes. They were completely self-sufficient. These monks learned philosophy as well as physical disciplines such as martial arts. One of the fathers who lived in the village decided to send one of his sons to the monastery. The father promised the monks that the boy would work very hard and obey them, and that he would work extra hard to repay their kindness through his labour and his contributions. The monks agreed, and the boy stayed, away from his family in the monastery. The first day the monks gave him a simple robe to wear and put him to work. 'Take that cauldron, fill it with water and place it on that large stone over there'. The boy did not understand the purpose, but he obeyed. There was no fire in the room so he wasn't sure what the cauldron was for. Then the monk said, 'Now splash the water out of the cauldron with your hands, like this'. This seemed very strange, but the boy obeyed him. Sometime later the stone floor was wet and the cauldron was empty, and his arms were stiff. Just then the monk came back and said, 'Now fill up the cauldron again'. He did this thrice on the first day, and repeated it thrice the next day. After a month, the boy was regretting his father's decision."

Yajus intervened, "Are you having a dig at me?"

Avyakta smiled and continued. "Finally, after three months, the boy was given a break to go and visit his family. He was very excited and felt relieved to be freed of his daily chore for a few days. At home, everyone kept asking, 'What did you learn? Did you learn martial arts? Can you break a board with your hands? What about meditation?' This made him uncomfortable because he hadn't really done anything. He had filled the cauldron and emptied it. That was about it. The boy became so angry that he yelled, 'I did not learn anything,' and he slammed his hand down on the thick wooden table. It instantly broke into two. Only then did he realise what he had learnt."

Avyakta took his son's hands into his and continued, "When you started practicing *pranayama*, your span of inhalation was four counts and exhalation five counts. Now..."

"Now I can do one breath cycle in about 44 counts," Yajus replied.

"Then where is the question of repetition, Yajus?" Avyakta asked.

With a little sternness in his voice, Avyakta continued, "Under the pretext of wanting to avoid boredom, monotony and repetition, using the context of change, variety, versatility and variation, you guys don't stick to anything long enough. When a seed stays rooted in the soil long enough, it will develop roots and eventually grow into a tree. However, if I keep unearthing the seed every few days and keep re-planting it in different places, it will not even become a plant."

Yajus's body language had changed. It was no more a son with his father. It was a seeker with a guru, hands folded in reverence and eyes filled with gratitude. The mind had turned into a blotting paper. He was completely receptive.

Avyakta said, "Expertise comes with time, but you don't stick to any job long enough. Precision comes with time, but you don't want to follow any process long enough. Perfection comes with time, but you are happy with superficial excellence. At the surface, it seems like the same *yogasana*; but, with every practice, the inner experience is higher and deeper. It seems like the same mantra and the same chanting, but the inner quietude is higher and deeper. The process may appear to be the same, but the experience never is. In growth, there are no repetitions. In repetition, there is only stagnation. Life is not about what you do; it is about the quality you bring to everything you do. If it isn't done long enough, the higher and deeper can never be experienced."

"Oh dad," Yajus intruded, "now I understand what do you mean when you say before enlightenment, the master was chopping wood and fetching water. After enlightenment too, he was chopping wood and fetching water. And the master remarked: enlightenment has not changed my actions, but has certainly changed the quality with which I perform my actions."

"True, my son," Avyakta elaborated, "the architect has to sketch for the rest of his life. The doctor has to place his stethoscope on the patient's chest for the rest of his life. The teacher has to go back to the class every year and start again, 'Newton's first law of motion is...' *Roti* and *dhal* has to be made in the kitchen for the rest of our lives... and son, you have to practice *pranayama* for the rest of your life. And yet, work has the power to become prayer; prayer has the power to become meditation; and meditation has the power to merge you with Him. The higher and the deeper can be experienced in everything. It all depends on the quality you bring to your actions rather than the action itself."

Avyakta concluded, "Boredom and monotony is because you think life is repetitive, but life in its very design cannot repeat itself. Life is always new. When a rose flower comes out, it is not a repetition of any rose flower that has preceded it. Nature always has a mystifying freshness to it. So Yajus, life need not change, but your outlook towards life needs to change. What you need isn't a new horizon, but new eyes to see the existing horizon. Wishing you most and more..."

Yajus has been with his father every day of his life, and yet, today seemed like the first day... the experience was higher and deeper.

The architect has to sketch for the rest of his life.
The doctor has to place his stethoscope on the patient's chest for the rest of his life.
The teacher has to go back to the class every year and start again, 'Newton's first law of motion is...'
Roti and *dhal* has to be made in the kitchen for the rest of our lives... and son, you have to practice *pranayama* for the rest of your life.
And yet, work has the power to become prayer; prayer has the power to become meditation; and meditation has the power to merge you with Him.
The higher and the deeper can be experienced in everything. It all depends on the quality you bring to your actions rather than the action itself.
What you need isn't a new horizon, but new eyes to see the existing horizon.

•••

A place for everything

A place for everything and everything in its place. A time for everything and everything in its time. That's about getting organised. First, the ability to define and then, the will to adhere to the defined. Once you experience the joy of organising things around you and living an organised life, only then will you know how much of a price we pay for living a disorganised life. Once you get organised in life, you never look lost. There is a flow about organised living.

T he parents bid a nervous goodbye. This was the first time their daughter was going to travel alone. She was going to celebrate Christmas with her grandparents at Goa. For Natasha, it was the excitement of flying alone at sixteen. Her 'Project Alone to Goa' was drawing a lot of attention from her relatives and she liked it. In fact, she had been bragging about it in her neighbourhood. It wasn't celebrating Christmas with her grandparents, but the adventure of flying alone that motivated Natasha to make this trip.

Most and more

With a boarding pass that read '29 B' in hand, chewing her bubble gum, Natasha walked through the aisle with arrogance that's exclusive to teenagers. She knew that her parents, like most adults, hated the very sight of the bubble being blown, but that was the very reason she liked bubble gum. It helped her get on other people's nerves effortlessly. It always got her the attention she wanted. She took '29 A' and started negotiating in her own mind... she would request whosoever the seat was allotted to, to sit in 'B' so that she could enjoy the view from the window. 'What if the person turns out to be a snob... no, I don't think so... not with a cute teenager like me...' her mind was a courtroom in itself. 'Is that the guy, is it this woman, oh no, not this fellow...' her mind kept guessing at people who walked through the aisle. How much unnecessary work our mind does, and how much it works without our even noticing that it works so much. 'This old man must be the guy' thought Natasha looking at a middle-aged man whose eyes were riveted on the 29th row. To show her displeasure at such adult company, she blew another bubble looking in his direction.

The man pushed his laptop bag into one of the overhead lockers, smiled at Natasha, and quietly occupied '29 B'. Some adult behaviour - not negotiating with a child for his window seat - not common behaviour though. People fight for their seat in an aircraft, even if it's just a 90-minute flight, as if they own it. Within minutes, the flight was in mid-air. Natasha kept alternating between looking through the window and glancing at the man seated next to her.

To put the kid at ease, the man stretched his hand out towards her. "Avyakta! Are you travelling all by yourself... brave little girl?"

"I am Natasha," she replied. "You are both right and wrong. I am brave, but I am not a little girl. I am sixteen." Avyakta broke into laughter and then added, "I am sorry dear. Anyway, how does it feel to be travelling alone?"

"It's exciting," Natasha replied. "I'm enjoying this journey alone. I am going to my grandparents' place. How about you? Why are you going to Goa?"

Avyakta replied, "I am an architect. I am doing a beach villa for one of my clients in Goa. The project is in its finishing stages and I am going for the final inspection. Natasha, what do you want to become in life?"

Meanwhile, it was breakfast time on the flight and the airhostess interrupted, "Vegetarian or non vegetarian?" "Non-vegetarian," said Natasha. "Vegetarian," was Avyakta's reply. Natasha disposed her bubble gum into a tissue. For the next few minutes, both of them were busy with their food trays. Not having got a reply from Natasha, Avyakta assumed that perhaps the little girl wasn't enjoying his company or the topic of discussion. So, he decided to leave the child in her own space. Again, simple but adult behaviour.

Natasha broke the silence. "I really like beautiful buildings. Is that your main job - to create buildings that look good and different?"

Avyakta took a sip of his lemon juice and then turned towards Natasha. "My job is three-fold - one, to define the spaces; two, to dress both the interiors and the exteriors; and three, to guide the most efficient execution of one and two. To the naked eye, like yours, the excitement is about the way the interiors and exteriors turn out... the look, the appearance. An architect is either a blessing or a curse to the one who executes the project, depending on how he assists them technically in the project execution. Personally, the greatness of an architect is characterised by his ability to define spaces. Am I making sense to you?"

"No," said Natasha emphatically. "It's interesting, but I don't follow you. What do you mean by defining spaces? If you think I won't be able to understand it, then leave it. I'll probably understand it when I reach that stage. Anyway, I'm not even sure if I want to become an architect."

"Well, let me see if I can explain this in a way that you can understand," Avyakta said. To communicate at the level at which the other would understand... again, an adult behaviour.

Avyakta said, "To put it simply, space definition is: 'A place for everything and everything in its place'. Take this breakfast tray, for example. A place for the main course and the main course in that place; a place for the bread and the bread in that place; a place for the butter, a place for the jam, a place for the juice and a place for the water... and everything in its place. If it was kept in any other way, you couldn't have kept all of this on this tray."

Avyakta took out his wallet from his pocket. "Look here," he said to Natasha, as he showed her his wallet. "A space for the notes, a space for the coins, a space for the credit cards, a space for the business cards... a place for everything and everything in its place. It's all about organising in the most optimum way."

Looking at eyes that confirmed interest and reflected understanding, Avyakta continued. "Natasha, so if I have to build a house for you, my most important responsibility is to take into consideration all your needs and wants, and see how I can define the spaces within the space available to achieve this objective... a place for everything and everything in its place."

Most and more

Natasha replied, "Shucks! I wish my father had hired you to build our house. In my house, everything lies everywhere. There isn't enough place for anything in my house and it always looks messy. I keep asking my father to build a bigger house, but he just doesn't listen to me."

Avyakta added, "A bigger place is not necessarily the solution. A bigger tray for this breakfast is not necessarily a solution; in fact, it will be a problem managing it in this small space. I suggest that you bring about a simple change in your lifestyle after you return home from your vacation. You'll see how much it can change your life. Decide where you want to leave your footwear. Make a decision and ensure that you will not leave your footwear anywhere else, under any circumstance. Divide your dressing table by defining clear spaces for the comb, the powder, hairbands, deodorants, etc... In the space that's available, define a space for everything and ensure that you keep everything in its place. Divide your wardrobe; even if it's just a shelf, define spaces for your school uniform, casual clothes, daily wear, etc... Define spaces in your school bag for books, notebooks, pens, etc... Rearrange the folders in your computer... use distinct and easily understandable names for your folders and organise all your files within those defined folders. You should be able to take your toothbrush and toothpaste from your bathroom shelf, even with your eyes closed. Even in the event of a power failure in your house, you should be able to take the tissues from the shelf in the right side corner of the room. With your eyes closed, you should be able to throw something into the dustbin in the left corner. You've decided to keep your cycle keys in a particular place; that's where you will keep them. No more the drama of searching for the keys every morning. No more creating a pandemonium in the house to search for your Maths notebook. A place for everything and everything in its place. Natasha, once you experience the joy of organising things around you and living an organised life, only then will you know how much of a price we pay for living a disorganised life. Once you get organised in life, you never look lost. There is a flow about organised living. Disorganised people look lost all the time, and with them everything gets lost. Even if an architect like me can define a place for everything, it's you who has to maintain everything in its place. So, it all boils down to being organised."

As the air hostess was clearing their trays, Natasha told Avyakta, "You're talking to me like you've known me for a very long time. True, you seem to be able to guess exactly what's happening in my life, especially the daily drama of the cycle keys. But I can tell you Mr.Avyakta, you've kindled a genuine interest in me to get myself organised."

Most and more

Avyakta added, "Natasha, this applies not only to space, but also to time. Getting organised is all about defining a time for everything and doing everything within that time. A time for exercise, a time for studies, a time for friends, a time for the family, a time for sports, a time for television, a time to go to sleep and a time to wake up... A time for everything, and everything in that time. There will be less wastage of time, better utilisation of it, a better balance to life, and above all, with the time available being a constant, a lot more will get accomplished. Natasha, I can carry over the same explanation to every possible resource. Getting organised is all about this: First, the ability to define and then, the will to adhere to the defined. An organised person is his own architect, and we can and should be our own architects for every resource available to us - space, time, finance, etc..."

The flight began its descent. Natasha popped another bubble gum into her mouth, fastened her seat belt and closed her eyes. Avyakta too closed his eyes. Minutes later, Natasha's voice made him open his eyes. "As all that you've said is beginning to seep in, I feel I should thank you for making a difference. You could have so easily been indifferent to me and travelled in your own space. Thanks for taking the effort and the initiative to make this little girl feel respected. Maybe, He, the architect, decided that me in 29 A and you in 29 B will travel together today and I will benefit from it. I will not let your words go waste. I still don't know if I want to be an architect by profession, but I will definitely be the architect of my own life. I will live a highly organised life."

"It was a pleasure travelling with you. God bless you! In whatever you wish to do, wishing you most and more... Can I borrow a bubble gum from you?" Avyakta took a bubble gum from Natasha and popped it into his mouth. He tried blowing a bubble, but in vain. He looked a little embarrassed, while Natasha beamed a smile that made the already beautiful girl look even more beautiful. Children love it when adults do what they like. Another adult behaviour from Avyakta... it's not that he wanted a bubble gum in his mouth; what he really wanted was a smile on Natasha's face.

A time for everything, and everything in that time. Then, there will be less wastage of time, a better balance to life, a lot more will get accomplished. Getting organised is all about the ability to define and then, the will to adhere to the defined. An organised person is his own architect, and we can be our own architects for every resource available to us - space, time, finance, etc...

● ● ●

Less will make it long

You say, "I like eating." Precisely for the
same reason, eat less. You will live long
enough to eat. You say, "I like sleeping."
Precisely for the same reason, sleep less.
You will live long enough to sleep. You
say, "I love her a lot." Precisely for the
same reason, give her space. Then alone
the relationship will survive the test of
time. You say, "I want to hit the top."
Precisely for the same reason, invest
enough time at the bottom to build the
base. Then the base will sustain you at the
top. Less will make it long. More will
make it short.

Against all odds

Mother earth is never benevolent to any seed. It does not make the process of germination easy for any seed. In fact, it stands against every seed. The seed has to sprout and fight against the forces of earth to emerge above the soil. Similarly, all great men were ordinary men who were forced by circumstances to meet great challenges. History is full of simple human beings who won over forces well beyond their control and emerged as Champions.

As far as the eyes could see, there was greenery stretched up to the mountains. The fresh air was healing and therapeutic. It was a small village, with its habitat untouched and un-invaded by urban civilisation. It was too small a paradise to be noticed by the likes of Columbus. "Ever since I moved to this place I am convinced that the heavens are not beyond these horizons," Avyakta wrote to his son.

After decades of relentless service, Avyakta woke up one morning to realise that he had almost become a public property. Everybody wanted his time and he was more than willing to share it for the betterment of others. He shared the same belief as echoed in the movie Spiderman II: "Intelligence is not a privilege but a gift. It must be used for the betterment of mankind." In the process of being there for everyone, Avyakta realised that he had not been there for himself. An inexplicable longing developed in him to be with himself. So he decided to take a sabbatical. Avyakta decided to go into a cocoon for a year, away from everything and everybody. He found a village in the mountains of Western Ghats and shifted base. With a box full of books and his clothes in a backpack, Avyakta entered this land that had more of nature and less of men.

After eleven months of unwinding, Avyakta was ready to go back and continue his mission of investing his intelligence for the betterment of others. But because his son meant so much to him, he felt that he too should experience the tranquillity of this wonderland. He invited his son to spend a week with him in the village, after which they could both return home.

Once a day, a bus passed through one of the nearby villages, about three kilometres away from Avyakta's paradise. Avyakta was at the bus stop, awaiting his son's arrival. On seeing the bus, Avyakta's eyes turned moist and his heart began to yearn to hug his son. As soon as his son got off the bus, the teenager with childlike exuberance dropped his bag on the ground, jumped onto his dad and hugged him tight. Time stood still for both of them. So lost were they in their embrace that no other world existed for them. Then they began the long walk to Avyakta's paradise. Avyakta's son went on and on; he had so much to say.

They had hardly walked a kilometre when the son began to grumble about the long walk. Avyakta smiled and said, "You are strange. You toil on a treadmill for sixty minutes, walk and walk and still reach nowhere, and yet feel so excited about it. Off the treadmill, even a walk of a few metres from the parking lot to a shopping mall calls for a big fuss. Enjoy the scenic beauty that surrounds you and celebrate every step you take. Cherish the fact that you are again in the presence of your father and appreciate the purity of the air you are inhaling. Let the face curve around the lips, not on the forehead. Come on, my boy! Keep pace with my old bones."

Avyakta's son smiled at him and said, "You know why we miss you so much. You make everything seem easy. In your presence, life is simple and effortless. Without you, life is truly a problem. I can't even begin to tell you how life has treated me in your absence."

Most and more

Avyakta chose not to say anything to his son and the two of them walked the distance to Avyakta's little shelter. Late in the evening, seated in front of the bonfire, with the majestic moon and millions of its glittering friends in the backdrop, Avyakta asked his son about his so-called problems and the cruelty with which life had treated him. "Did you experience earthquakes, cyclonic storms, floods, riots, terminal illness, paralysing accidents, etc... what sort of problems, my dear son?" Avyakta asked sarcastically.

Understanding that his dad was having a dig at him, Avyakta's son glared at him and again turned his gaze to the blazing fire. Avyakta continued. "We are meeting after a very long separation and so I do not wish to say anything to upset you. But I expect my son to live his life with greater maturity. With your permission, I would like to share some of my thoughts."

It was one of those typical situations where one's ego doesn't want to hear anything, but the curiosity gets the better of it... His son nodded his head slightly. Avyakta moved his chair a little closer to his son and said, "Human ego thrives on the fairy tales it creates about the problems of life. Despite what our ego cons us into believing, the majority of our problems are optional. Most of what we call problems, small or big, is self-created. You choose to have a problem when you notice the little red light on your dashboard blinking, but postpone taking the car for the oil change. You may get upset when the car stops midway in peak-hour traffic, but it won't change the fact that what you are facing now is a self-created problem. While spending beyond your means, while overusing your credit cards, you are creating a future problem for yourself. We are aware that when we repeatedly postpone the nurturing of the most important relationships in our life, problems of resentment or even estrangement will eventually arise. We allow little challenges and inconveniences to grow into upsetting and unnecessary problems everyday."

To his son who was now looking at him and no longer pretending to look at the bonfire to avoid eye contact, Avyakta said, "Of course, problems like natural calamities and unexpected terminal illness may be beyond an individual's control. But most of the other issues are self-created. The forest fire we face today is the little spark we overlooked yesterday. Most of today's problems are yesterday's challenges overlooked."

"My son," Avyakta said, "if you want to raise your life to legendary heights, then you must be prepared to face bigger challenges. If you wish to set bigger goals and gear up to face greater challenges, then you must first overcome these trivial, everyday disturbances. These day-to-day trivialities rob you of your energy. With a little consistency of lifestyle, some discipline and systematic living, most of these habitual trifles can be overcome."

Avyakta's son got out of his chair and sat on the ground, with his back resting against Avyakta's legs. It made him feel a little closer to his dad. "Just listening to you is enough for me dad. I don't even have to eat; I just forget my world." Wrapping his son in his arms, Avyakta continued.

"First, give up the freedom with which you use the word 'problem'. Understand that there is a world of difference between a problem and a challenge. If I am confronted by a lion in the middle of a jungle, and am unarmed, then I have a problem. But, if I have a machine gun with me, then it is the lion that has a problem. I just have the challenge of firing the gun in time. So remember, when the situation I confront is greater than the resources I have, then it can be termed as a problem. However, if the resources I have are greater than the situation I am faced with, then it is just a challenge. I just have to manage my resources properly to overcome the situation. Most of the time, man sees life as a problem because he does not take stock of the available resources with which he can overcome the situation. Human predicament is that we overestimate our problems and underestimate our ability to trounce them."

Under the pretext of wanting to have a glass of water, Avyakta left his son alone by the bonfire. He wanted him to meditate upon what he had heard. While words provide knowledge, it is during moments of silence and contemplation that they turn into wisdom. Information is nothing more than mental garbage if it doesn't transform an individual.

When Avyakta returned, he brought a bottle of water for his son. Just as an unexpected service initiative builds customer loyalty in business, every unanticipated demonstration of affection strengthens the bond of love in personal relationships. With a warm 'Love you dad', Avyakta's son took a few gulps of water.

Avyakta added, "Life's challenges aren't there to stifle you. In fact, they serve you and help you to discover who you are. Challenges actually oblige you; for, when conquered, they help you to chase greater challenges and in turn provide you greater growth. As a child, when you began to crawl, your mother used to place a toy a little away from you and challenge you to reach for it. Every time you were about to lay your hands on the toy, she would move it further away from you. Was that an act of cruelty or was it an act of love, to play the role of a catalyst in your growth? When you began to take your first tiny steps, your mother would always stand a little away from you and challenge you to reach out to her. True, sometimes you fell and hurt yourself, but isn't that part of the process of growing up? Similarly, Existence always challenges her favourite creation - man, so that he can discover the stuff he is made of."

The breeze stopped abruptly, as if the trees around wanting to listen to Avyakta had told it to keep quiet. The bonfire looked even more beautiful with its flame steady in the absence of the wind. Why the moon felt shy at the turn of events is beyond even a poet's imagination, as she used the cover of clouds to hide her face.

Avyakta yawned and said, "Excuse me, my son. I think we should have dinner and go to sleep. I just want you to think about this before you go to sleep. If the British hadn't ruled India, life would never have provided the context for the barrister to discover the Mahatma Gandhi within him. But for the impoverished and those dying on the streets, the schoolteacher wouldn't have discovered the Mother Teresa within her. Without apartheid, history would have lost Nelson Mandela. But for oppression, the world wouldn't have known the legendary Martin Luther King. But for the exploitation of the common man in the name of religion, we would have missed Jesus Christ. If human beings hadn't been in such a quandary, a Buddha wouldn't have emerged. But for Ravana, Rama wouldn't have met Hanuman; and but for Duryodhana, there would be no Bhagavad-Gita. When Krishna says, 'Whenever *adharma* (moral degeneration) is at its peak, the Lord incarnates', please understand my son, even *adharma* is only an opportunity for the Lord to descend."

"Do you know son," Avyakta said, "that Mother earth is never benevolent to any seed? It does not make the process of germination easy for any seed. In fact, it stands against every seed. The seed has to sprout and fight against the forces of the earth to emerge above the soil. Providential it is that the very earth, which stood against the seed till it sprouted, then nurtures it, and helps it grow. It is nature's way of qualifying the seed; if found deserving, it provides all the resources that are needed for it to grow to its full potential. The seeds that fail to rise against the earth die and turn dust unto dust."

Avyakta got up from his chair and said, "Similarly, all great men were ordinary men who were forced by circumstances to meet great challenges. History is full of simple human beings who won over forces well beyond their control and emerged as champions."

Most and more

Avyakta walked in to set the dinner on the table. His son realised why God had created a world of raw materials and left it to man to make the finished goods... unpainted canvasses, unsung music and unresolved challenges... and in completing them, man discovers the stuff he is made of. The breeze resumed, the moon came out, and the fire began to dance. They didn't know yet that Avyakta would soon be leaving them behind. He was going back to being public property once again, for there was another world that needed to be transformed into Heaven.

There is a world of difference
between a problem and a challenge.
If I am confronted by a lion in the middle of a
jungle, and am unarmed, then I have a problem.
But, if I have a machine gun with me,
then it is the lion that has a problem.
So, when the situation I confront is greater than
the resources I have, then it can be termed as a
problem. However, if the resources I have are
greater than the situation I am faced with,
then it is just a challenge.
Human predicament is that
we overestimate our problems
and underestimate our ability to trounce them.

Beyond the finishing line

When you are about to give up, that's the exact point to hold on. That's the point to go beyond the finishing line. When you think it is over, that's the point to carry on. When you think of stopping, that's the point to move on. When you think it is the end, that's the point to go on. Going beyond the finishing line, in every endeavour of yours and in every path you choose to walk. With staying power, every end becomes a bend. Keep on keeping on.

Three vehicles were almost converging, but the black SUV pulled into the last vacant slot in the parking lot, just ahead of the other two. The other cars missed the slot in a matter of seconds, which meant those drivers would have to park their cars in the nearby lane and walk back about 200 metres to get to the gym. Man is sometimes a riddle unto himself. The same guy who would go on to walk a few kilometres on the treadmill in the gym frets about having to walk 200 metres to the gym. With a grin aroused by a sense of cheap victory, Arpita emerged from her SUV. How often such little thrills make us feel like Olympians!

Arpita soon entered the changing room in the gym and changed into her workout clothes. The cardio section of the gym was really crowded. All the six treadmills, the four cross-trainers and the three cycles were in use, and it came as no surprise. It was just the first week of January and this was an after-effect of 'New Year Resolutions'. Arpita's face blossomed into a broad smile on spotting Avyakta. Seeing Avyakta exercise in the gym with such religious consistency at fifty was one of the greatest motivations for this twenty-two-year-old girl.

"How is your business doing?" enquired Avyakta. Arpita had started a diet kitchen a year ago, hoping that her innovative concept of a health-food joint would take off and become the talk of the town. Much before she could open her mouth to speak, her expression communicated that things weren't okay. "We are yet to break even. I have left no stone unturned, but nothing seems to be working. Perhaps, I am not cut out for business. Every new idea and new strategy seems exciting at the thought level, but when implemented it doesn't yield the expected results. It is beginning to ruffle my ego. I had fought tooth and nail with everyone in the family saying that I had an enterprising idea at hand. They didn't want me to get into business. I thought I would have the last laugh, but now they are laughing at me." Her dimples were her trademark, but before she completed her last sentence her dimples and her smile had faded out.

Just then, two adjacent treadmills became available. As Arpita and Avyakta nodded at each other and got on to them, the two who had gone to park their cars in the adjacent lane entered the cardio section. Just missed... once again. The dimples were back on Arpita's face... she was all smiles though Avyakta couldn't understand what she was so amused about. Three minutes on the treadmill, Avyakta began to jog. Inspired by seeing the fifty-year-old jog, a couple of minutes later, Arpita who normally restricted herself to brisk walking also started jogging. In a matter of five minutes, Arpita was gasping for breath and showed signs of wanting to resume brisk walking. Avyakta urged her, "Arpita, go on... go on... two more minutes." She couldn't but heed to the words of a man she had so much respect for. She went on for two more minutes. Avyakta again exhorted, "Arpita good... very good... you have got into the rhythm... don't lose this momentum... carry on... three more minutes... just three more minutes... listen to your mind... it wants you to go on..."

In life, most people reach where they reach because someone who cares for them helps them to see further. Arpita just needed that push. Eight, nine, ten, that's it... eleven, twelve, thirteen... Arpita, on her own volition,

---

Most and more

carried on for twenty minutes. An hour later, when Arpita was walking towards the changing room after her workout, she noticed Avyakta waiting for her in the juice bar. He gestured to Arpita to come and take the seat next to him. With Arpita's approval, Avyakta ordered for two glasses of 'carrot-beetroot-peppermint' juice.

Arpita was still wiping her sweat. Avyakta rested his elbow on the table, and placing his chin on the palm of his hands, looked at Arpita and said, "You were a student till a few years ago. Have you gone through this experience during night studies? There is a point at which you feel very sleepy and if you somehow manage to stay awake even for a few minutes beyond that point... you no longer feel sleepy. In fact, you feel so fresh that you find it difficult to sleep after that." Arpita nodded her head vigorously.

Avyakta continued, "Have you also gone through this experience... you come home famished. You are almost being consumed by your own hunger. You ask mummy to give you some food. Mummy takes just a few minutes to get things ready; but, to you the wait seems eternal. You are on the verge of developing stomach cramps. Just then, the doorbell rings and you answer it. You find one of your best friends at the door. You invite her to join you at the dinning table, but she declines your offer. So, you sit with her in your living room and she leaves thirty minutes later after having discussed everything under the sun. Wonder of wonders, you are no longer hungry; in fact, you are in no mood to eat." "Of course," acknowledged Arpita.

Avyakta further enquired, "Have you also gone through this experience… you went to a party and people were already on the dance floor. Others forced you and you reluctantly joined the dance. After a few minutes of dancing, you felt a little drained and decided to stop. Just then the DJ played your favourite number and you decided to dance for just one more number, and that's it… after that you just couldn't stop dancing. After a point, you were no more feeling drained but instead energised, so much so that you no more had the heart to leave the dance floor."

Two glasses of 'carrot-beetroot-pepper-mint' juice had been placed on the table, but neither was even looking at it. Arpita was nodding and smiling in acknowledgement. He added, "Even today, when you were on the treadmill, did you notice that there was a point when you wanted to stop? But you managed to carry on and once you crossed that point you could go on much longer than what you believed was possible."

Arpita now rested her elbow on the table and her chin in the palm of her hands and tilted her face towards

Avyakta. Avyakta gently leaned back on the chair, folded his hands across his chest and continued. "It is a law... an Existential law. Life creates an imaginary finishing line on your path. This is life's way of differentiating mediocrity from the rest. Every mediocre accepts the imaginary finishing line as the finishing line and stops at it. The champion few alone go beyond the imaginary finishing line. Life always holds its abundance just beyond that imaginary finishing line. A paradise awaits us with open arms just beyond the imaginary finishing line. Hold on a little longer... do not accept what seems to be the finishing line. Life sets a trap for all of us on every path we tread. This is her way of discriminating the 'also-rans' from the champions. The mediocre takes it to be the finishing line and stops. The legend knows that if he can just go beyond this imaginary finishing line, then there are no more finishing lines."

"Arpita," Avyakta emphatically added, "the magic and miracles of life always unfold just beyond that imaginary finishing line. Why alone the examples of night studies, hunger, dancing, running... even with relationships. Sometimes, a relationship that you cherish so much reaches a threshold... it appears as though everything is going to fall apart. Even if one among the two involved in the relationship can just hold on a little longer, the same relationship will touch depths that will defy imagination. While writing poetry, the poet reaches a point when the next line does not flow. His mind goes blank. A good poet knows that if he can hold on just a little longer to get the next line of his poem, the perennial flow will once again take over. It is the question of one more word for a communicator, one more stroke for the painter, one more day for the businessman, Arpita... one more day. When you are about to give up... that's the exact point to hold on. That's the point to go beyond the finishing line. When you think it is over... that's the point to carry on... when you think of stopping... that's the point to move on... when you think it is the end... that's the point to go on. Going beyond the finishing line, in every endeavour of yours and in every path you choose to walk. With staying power, even end becomes a bend."

By then, Arpita was feeling so connected to Avyakta that there was not only communication between the two of them, but also a communion of vibrations. Arpita was beginning to draw Avyakta's vibrations.

Avyakta said, "My child, this is the 'beyond the finishing line' law at the micro level. When the same phenomenon is expanded to a macro level, it becomes the law of 'critical mass'. When a certain critical number achieves certain awareness, this new awareness gets communicated from mind to mind. When only a limited number of people know of a new way, it remains the conscious property of the few. But there is a point at which even if only one more person tunes in to this new awareness, a field is strengthened so that this awareness is picked up by almost everyone! Humanity at that point will go through a dramatic and collective shift in consciousness. It happens when the critical mass for a shift is reached. The world undergoes a spiritual renaissance when a certain number of spiritually awakened individuals are reached. Haven't we seen that happen with social networking websites? Quantitative change brings about a qualitative change. Whether it is ideas or products or messages or behaviour... at the point of critical mass, it just spreads like a virus... as if a thought epidemic has happened. Beyond that point, growth is always in Geometric progression. The point of critical mass just beyond the finishing line is that magic moment when it all begins to spread like wildfire... everything changes all at once. I wish you most and more... and Arpita, you will experience most and more in every aspect of your life, if you keep looking beyond the imaginary finishing lines."

Avyakta and Arpita walked towards their parking lots. Avyakta, as he opened his car door, looked at Arpita and said, "With one dot (.), it means the end. Add two more dots to it (...), and now it means 'so on and so forth', a continuity. Keep on keeping on."

Filtering Times

The bullet that had left the gun cannot return to the gun. It has to hit the target. A venture begun should be a venture accomplished. Whether something is a stepping stone or a stumbling block depends on how you use it. *Charaiveti, Charaiveti.* It means, "Go on. Go on. Do not halt. Do not stagnate. Endeavour continuously. Don't stop. Rest not. Go on. Keep going on."

"Happy Morning! How are you?" "Oh, I am on Top of the World!"

"How are you doing?" "Happy! I am very happy. And, I love you so much."

"Hey, how is life treating you?" "Of course, rocking. I am only processing expansion. Only thinking growth. I have never been in such form. Just rocking, my dear."

This was the typical language and expression that one would hear and experience when people of this fraternity met. But things had changed in the land that Columbus had discovered. The tremors are always felt way beyond the epicentre of the quake.

Most and more

Miles and miles away, days and days later, the aftershocks continue. Didn't an earthquake in some part of the world result in the terrible tsunami in so many other parts of the world? More people died elsewhere than at the source of destruction. Though the epicentre of this economic-quake was in that 'land of opportunities', the rest of the world was feeling the tremors, because the world had shrunk into an economic global village.

Man's only fallback, God, has but a cruel sense of humour. His *leela* doesn't necessarily make man laugh. Sometimes, His *leela* makes man cry. But then, there is no point in asking why the scores are 15, 30 and then 40? There's absolutely no point in asking, for those are the rules and that's how tennis is played. Why 64 squares in a chessboard? Why 18 holes in a golf course? How come 22-yards is universal, but the boundary line changes according to whims and fancies in cricket. There is no point in asking any of these questions. Ardent followers of the game will call you a fool for questioning the rules of the game. If this is the case with manmade games, what's there to speak about His games? He has this cruel sense of humour in playing His *leela* in ways that man is tested and challenged, time and again, and again. It is futile to question the game. Instead, learn the rules of the game, master the game, play it well, and win the game. Man has to have this faith about His game that the end is always beautiful and it is in man's favour. Know from the beginning that the end is always beautiful. Have this faith that no parent will ever give his child a story to read if it doesn't have a happy ending, and play the game of life courageously.

Right now, the phrases and the emotions of the people of this fraternity were sounding very different. "Tough times." "We had to lay off 100 of them." "We are feeling the pinch." "I am seeing my dreams crumble right in front of my eyes." These phrases were very new to this fraternity. However, when my neighbour's house is on fire, I cannot help but feel nervous. Like how physical diseases can be infectious, psychological gloom is also contagious. With so much interchange of gloomy thoughts and negative languaging, even those who were not directly affected were beginning to lose their mental focus, intellectual poise and emotional centeredness. What cannot be avoided must be endured. When flight isn't an option, fight we must. A lifeboat was needed. Avyakta arrived. People settled down around him. He smiled and said, "I don't have a magic wand to change everything, but I do have a walking stick, which will give us the support and the strength to stand up and move on."

Most and more

Avyakta said, "We have enjoyed good times. We have to endure these tough times. I promise you that we will experience wonderful times. In ancient Rome, a person would hold a laurel wreath over Caesar's head and from time to time say the words, 'Thou art mortal'. The purpose was to remind the man with such great powers that he too, after all, was only a man, and as such, mortal. I think we should stop playing God and understand in times like these that we do not have all the answers. We are mortals, and mortals have all the questions but not necessarily all the answers. Falling is not failing. The drive to 'Go on' has brought us to this point and the drive to 'Go on' will take us from here. Everything came down after one sunset. Everything will go up after one sunrise. Keep going in search of that one sunrise after which everything will change. One more day... one more time... just put that one foot in the front on what seems like an endless road with no destination in sight. Every man who has walked this planet, and humanity as a whole, at various periods in history, has encountered a point in life when the going seemed futile, was suffocated by events and situations, when the only thing that seemed possible was to sit in the middle of the road and let the world and everything pass by. Today, we understand why we went through what we went through yesterday. Likewise, tomorrow we will understand what and why we went through what we went through today."

First-aid cannot cure the injury, but it does arrest deterioration. The treatment will take its course. Years of inadequacies in global systems cannot be set right in a day. What does it take to reach the top of Mount Everest? What does it take to fall from there? If we understand that difference, then we will understand that the rise is always time-consuming and the fall is always instantaneous. Avyakta was just rendering psychological first-aid. The game of life is tough, but it isn't a game that cannot be won. Some in the audience were sitting with such heavy hearts that they couldn't even comprehend what Avyakta was saying. So often, people who need the solution the most heed to it the least. How true it is that growth is not taught, but caught. Yet, there were others who were nodding their heads in agreement and exchanging, 'I understand' glances at each other.

Avyakta clarified, "I don't want to call these bad times, for I see them as 'Filtering' times. What is cultivated is called a crop. What grows by itself is a weed. The crop is a result and effect of human sweat. In a good economy, everybody makes money. In a bad economy, only the good makes money. It is during times like these that you come to know what you are made of.

Are you a crop or a weed? Investments were yielding more than what work could. So, work was beginning to lose its dignity. Work plus investments is very good for the economy. But when investments start replacing work, it spells doom for an economy. Money was making so much money that human ability, competence, education, leadership, experience, expertise and systematic development of organisations were all beginning to lose their value. If everybody becomes prosperous by winning lotteries, then what sanctity will work have? What we were experiencing was not necessarily a rise in the standard of life through money earned by hard work. What we were going through was a credit card economy, a borrowed economy - an economy where the common man's borrowing was disproportionate to what he was capable of earning and returning - I call it the economy of 'False' money. I call it the economy of 'Imaginary' money. A correction was required, and the correction is happening."

There were little smiles here and there. Defining the problem is the beginning of solving it. Avyakta added, "Humanity has been built on certain virtues like commitment, resilience, determination, honesty, loyalty, integrity and the willingness to sweat to arrive. There was a time when managements exploited employees. That was wrong. We have just gone through times when employees used organisations as transitory grounds to enhance their resume and trade higher pay packets. This too is wrong. The one providing the bread and the one earning the bread have to work in a win-win arrangement. A correction was required and the correction is happening. Good times shield the non-productive. Bad times filter them. Filtering is happening. We are being tested, but the good will never be forsaken. More than ever, this is the time for you to be strong and to believe in yourself. A person carrying a heavy load is fine as long as he keeps moving. The minute he stops, the load gets heavier and the distance to be travelled seems greater. The longer you put off something that you should do, the more difficult it becomes to get started. So, keep moving. Even if you have to slow down, slow down; but, keep moving. Life is just separating the wheat from the chaff. If you are good enough, just keep marching... roses await you beyond the thorns. It's okay for you to feel tired, but do not stop. By refusing to accept life's reverse gear, we throw ourselves in Top Gear."

Avyakta said, "Sri Krishna said, 'Hey *Bhaarata* (Arjuna), whenever in the passage of time, *dharma* is weakened or is under attack; whenever *adharma* spreads without control, it is then that I reincarnate myself with all my powers to restore Faith.' My dear friends, I think

God caught us a little unaware. Little did I think that He would use the context of a bad economy to bring about the correction! We have enjoyed good times. We have to endure these tough times. And, I promise you that we will experience wonderful times."

What's expected from a leader isn't solace, but solutions. What people need is not consolation, but the motivation to prod on... Avyakta empowered his fraternity by telling them, "The bullet that had left the gun cannot return to the gun. It has to hit the target. A venture begun should be a venture accomplished. Whether something is a stepping stone or a stumbling block depends on how you use it. The sages who gave us the Upanishads say, '*Charaiveti, Charaiveti*'. Buddha used to end all his discourses saying, '*Charaiveti, Charaiveti*' meaning, 'Go on. Go on. Do not halt. Do not stagnate. Endeavour continuously. Don't stop. Rest not. Go on. Keep going on. *Charaiveti, Charaiveti.* Seek most and more... and settle for nothing less than most and more...'"

The mind of the man is the man. Change the mind and you have changed the man. That day, something changed within them in experiencing Avyakta. The effect of that internal change will manifest sooner than later.

It's not somehow! It is how?

The unwillingness to be the flagship, the reluctance to assume responsibility, and shying away from leadership are grave deterrents to what one can do with one's abilities. The better you are, the more you can use yourself at the top. The better you are, the more effective you can be at the top. So, seek to be a leader and not a mere follower.

Nothing is as sweet as success. Nothing is as bitter as failure. This is one organisation which has tasted both, and they now know the difference. The previous financial year was a fiasco, but this year was sensational. The memories of the annual review meeting of the previous year were still vivid in the minds of the employees who had stayed with the organisation, in spite of the tough times the organisation had gone through. Some stayed out of helplessness, some out of hope, and many out of their faith in Avyakta, the Chief Belief Officer (CBO) of the organisation.

Concluding the review meeting last year, to a room filled with drooping shoulders, Avyakta had said,

"This year we stand defeated. Success isn't what we achieve compared to others, but what we achieve compared to what we are capable of. To move at a snail's pace is success to the snail, but not to the rabbit. Of course, the inability to move at a rabbit's pace isn't a snail's failure. The heartache is that we will not do what we were capable of. That is why I say we have defeated ourselves. We did not lose to our competition; we lost to ourselves. I take the onus of responsibility for this debacle. It was a leadership failure. What's over is over. We needed a wake-up call, and this was it. The ego of the organisation is hurt. Collective fear is courage. Collective hurt is the seed of a revolution. Now the key is to channelize this hurt into performance. Success is the greatest moral revenge. You can smell the rain much before it comes. I smell success. It's coming. As we march into the next financial year, I want all of you to know that 'When a winner loses, he always comes back to be a better winner'. In my heart, I have visualised the end. In my mind, I have seen the path. This time we will make it."

Of course, they made it. It was the next annual review meeting. There was a spring in everyone's step. Every organisation has its share of winners and also-rans. The success of leadership lies in ensuring that the winners outnumber the also-rans. While a few cannot carry the load of many, many can always make up for the few. This time the meeting appeared to be a congregation of winners. One after another, every employee went up the dais and reviewed his personal performance. Applause and standing ovations were the tune of the day. It was celebrations galore. Isn't celebration the *raga* of success?

In the entire organisation, there were just seven people who did not qualify to be called champion performers. They too were asked to go up the dais and share their feelings. Five among the seven attempted to justify and rationalise their failure. Cursed souls! Perhaps they didn't realise that the attempt to justify failure is an invitation to more failures. Explanations and justifications of failure are like a pain balm that may relieve the pain but can never remove the scar.

When Avyakta said in the previous year's meeting, 'When a winner loses, he always comes back to be a better winner', he was referring to the category of people who channelize the hurt of failure into a resolve to succeed. The other two belonged to this category. Their eyes turned red the moment they went up the dais. They didn't delve much on the year that had gone by, but kept harping on the year ahead. Their body language, the clenched fist, the slapping of palms, the nodding of the head, not sideways (negating) but up and down (affirming), and above all, the unspoken message from their eyes - all expressed the fire of their conviction to succeed. Apart from everything else they spoke, both of them said one thing in common, "I will somehow make it to the champion's category next year. I do not know how, but I somehow want to make it." Both the times when this was said, Avyakta smiled at the speaker, and anyone who knew Avyakta knew that there was a deeper meaning to the smile. When a smile is not a mere facial gymnastics or corporate etiquette, but a spontaneous flowering, it is always a reflection of very deep thoughts and feelings.

The meeting ended with a short address from Avyakta. "Congrats! All of us deserve this moment. Still, a word of caution! Success isn't about going to the top but it is about staying on top. Success isn't a one-time accomplishment, but the consistency of it. Last year, most of you discovered how good you are. This year, endeavour to make yourselves better. Let us raise our own standards, both as individuals and as an organisation. This year, I am going to give all of you new goals to achieve besides numbers."

Then, as if he wanted them to ponder over the suspense, he created an intentional pause by reaching for a glass of water. There was a mix of excitement and restlessness in the room. To the congregation that was waiting with rapt attention, Avyakta said,

"The greatest pitfall of today's corporate world is the underutilisation of human potential by incompetent and immature leadership. So, what is the solution? More and more of you should go in search of corporate environments, which will allow you to exercise your leadership capabilities. More and more of you should come forward to assume leadership. Having said this, I shall provide you with the environment to exercise your leadership capabilities in the coming year. An organisation with good players keeps adding to its success. An organisation with good leaders keeps multiplying its success. My goal for you is that I would like to see a lot of you grow into leaders. Unlike sports, an organisation is blessed; for, it has the scope for many leaders."

Avyakta asked, "Why would a genius choose to be a follower instead of a leader? If Bill Gates was led by someone else; if JRD Tata didn't have a decision-making chair; if Mahatma Gandhi was a follower; if Mother Teresa was led by any other mortal; if Richard Bach was a stenographer... history would not be what it is. The unwillingness to be the flagship, the reluctance to assume responsibility, and shying away from leadership are grave deterrents to what one can do with one's abilities. The better you are, the more you can use yourself at the top. The better you are, the more effective you can be at the top. So, seek to be a leader and not a mere follower. The unnoticed and unrecorded tragedy of our world is the number of geniuses we have missed for want of effective leadership, and the disinclination of these geniuses to assume leadership."

The shepherd not only rejoices the return of ninety-nine of his sheep, but also feels concerned about the one that hasn't returned. So, Avyakta approached the two who had displayed great determination and took them to his cabin. Noticing their nervousness, Avyakta eased them by saying, "I appreciate the strength of your resolve. The reason I wanted to talk to you is because I see promise in you. Both of you said, 'I do not know how, but I somehow want to make it'. If you don't know 'how', then you won't be able to make it. The difference between wishful thinking and a goal is this: In wishful thinking you don't know the 'how'; with a goal you have defined the 'how'. Would you believe if Edmund Hillary said, 'I just kept walking and somehow landed at the top of Mt. Everest'? Would you believe if Sam Walton said, 'I just kept coming to office everyday and just kept working hard and one day to my surprise we hit the top'? Would you believe a bricklayer if he said, 'I just kept placing one brick over another and accidentally ended up putting this monumental structure together'? Don't you know that Edmund Hillary would have chalked out a plan - not just one, but also a Plan-B and a Plan-C and may be even a Plan-D, in case Plan-A failed. Don't you know that Sam Walton continuously worked and reworked his business plans, over and over again, year after year, till one of his strategies clicked? And I am sure he is still working on improving it. Don't you know that the brilliance of an architect would have preceded the work of the bricklayer? My dear guys, success is never 'somehow', but is always 'how'."

To put them at ease and to give them the time to mentally digest what had been spoken, Avyakta offered them a cup of tea. He said, "Enjoy your tea and I will continue later." To give them the space to think, he intentionally walked out of his office, leaving them to themselves. It is not what people hear, but it is what they deliberate over after listening, that gets internalised. As a CBO, Avyakta's job profile was to mentor people to have faith in themselves and believe in what they do. So, he intuitively knew that people have to be given time for realisations to sink in.

Avyakta returned after a while. He warmly patted them on their back, took his seat and continued. "Planning the details of the process in order to achieve a result is like creating a good route map. Having the right map does not necessarily confirm that we will always stay on track, but it will serve as a guide when we go off track. So it is when you plan the details of the process. So many people say, 'I do not plan because things seldom go as per plan'. To know that things are not going the way they should be going needs a plan. A student who plans his studies always performs better than the one who 'somehow' wants to do well. An employee who has a plan for the day is more efficient than the one who makes it to office and then wonders what to do. It is much easier to make corrections at the level of blueprint than at the level of structure. Similarly, planning the 'how' - the details of the process - will enable you to provide for contingencies much better than during the execution of the process. Everyone desires success but everyone does not succeed, and the difference is rather simple and obvious - does he have the 'how' on paper before putting his best foot forward? People who fail to plan are planning for a failure."

"To conclude," Avyakta said, "That is why I always say, 'My heart has seen the end and my mind has seen the path'. The heart desires the goal and now the mind has to lay out the process of 'how'. The heart will always scream out - 'somehow', and believe me, every heart screams. What it needs is a prudent mind that can think and find an answer to the 'how'. Hey guys, I know your heart is ready. Now put your mind to work. And remember, the better you are, the more effective you can be at the top. Aim for the top. Wishing you most and more..."

We won't abuse million bucks, will we? Yet, how often, we waste some advices, which are truly priceless, by not internalising them into our lives. Will the two of them, use it or abuse it, only time will tell.

**In wishful thinking you don't know the 'how';
with a goal you have defined the 'how'.
Planning the details of the process in order to
achieve a result is like creating a good route map.
Having the right map does not necessarily confirm
that we will always stay on track, but it will serve
as a guide when we go off track. So it is when you
plan the details of the process. A student who
plans his studies always performs better than the
one who 'somehow' wants to do well.
An employee who has a plan for the day is more
efficient than the one who makes it to office and
then wonders what to do.
Everyone desires success but everyone does not
succeed, and the difference is rather simple and
obvious: Does he have the 'how' on paper before
putting his best foot forward?
People who fail to plan are planning for a failure.**

Most and more

● ● ●

Good people should be rich

Money, in the hands of a good human being will be used to create a better world, while the same in the hands of an evil-minded human being will be used to destroy the existing world. The only way to vanquish bad from the world is to make bad people financially poor. The only way to achieve that is by ensuring good people become financially rich. So, every good human being has the moral responsibility to be rich.

Situational Leadership

Leadership is a cruel game. You have to complete the puzzle, but all the pieces are not with you. So your success no more depends solely on you, and yet, anyone's failure is your failure. Simply put, in academics, answers are question dependent; but in leadership, solutions are situation dependent. The leader who leads by the philosophy that there are no 'no solution' situations is the leader of the future.

He was the pride of every teacher. His grasp, his retention and his recall were incomparable. It was no wonder that he was a state rank holder in his board exams, the topper in Indian Institute of Technology and had just passed out among the top ten from the Indian Institute of Management, Ahmedabad. He had a range of choices when it came to choosing his first employer, but the patriotic citizen decided to stay in the soil that had nurtured him. He was joining work as a Product Manager in an Indian company that had gone global. Ved and Avyakta sat in the balcony, sipping a cup of tea. Greenery all round, chirping birds, passing clouds, cool breeze, expansive space -

all this would have created a poetic setting, but the reality was a small 6'x4' balcony overlooking the road. There was intermittent traffic noise, but one tends to get so accustomed to certain noises that they cease to be a disturbance any more. Nothing dreamy about the setting, but this was certainly going to be the beginning of a dream.

More than your own success, the success of people you have groomed gives you greater satisfaction. To Avyakta, it was a moment of parental pride. Ved was everything a father would want of his son. The son exclaimed to the father, "*Appa*, you seem to be more nervous than I am!"

Avyakta replied, "It is not fear of failure Ved, but the anxiety for excellence. You have pampered our expectations with your results. You have raised the bar of expectations. Nothing but the best from you is acceptable. I know you will, but..."

Ved intervened, "I know *Appa*, every successful student is not necessarily a success in his life. What is it that I need to know that I couldn't have learnt at school?"

Avyakta waved to the children in a passing school bus. Simple, costless luxuries! Children always respond, and inexplicably any response from a child brings a smile to the lips. Ved carried the empty teacups to the kitchen sink. To ask a question and wait peacefully for the answer, without getting desperate or restless - isn't that a professional virtue by itself? When Ved returned, Avyakta said, "The platform of life isn't tailor-made. The setting isn't perfect. In academics you had to outperform others, but now you have to perform with others. In academics you had to compete, but now you have to make things complete. Leadership is a cruel game. You have to complete the puzzle, but all the pieces are not with you. So, your success no more depends solely on you, and yet, others' failure is your failure too. Simply put, in academics, answers are question dependent; but in leadership, solutions are situation dependent. Leadership isn't about the chair, position, reports, ratios, adulation, perks and benefits... but it is about prudence. It lies in the ability to win in unexpected situations, to be smart in the moments of need, to empower others, to be creative when no solution seems apparent... basically to feel in control of the situation."

"*Amma* hasn't been to college, nor been through any leadership training," Avyakta added. "But she is a master at situational leadership. Each one of us in the family is so different, and our tastes are just as varied. She knows how to manage (read manipulate) the resources in the kitchen and serve the same dish in different flavours and finishes, and satisfy all of us. Yet, I see everyday in professional life, so-called professionals getting paranoid when expectations deviate from the prescribed norms. Habitual thinkers that they are, most of them struggle to think outside the box. Now we are enjoying financial abundance, but even at a time when I was earning only one-tenth of what I am earning now, *Amma* managed the family's needs and still provided for all within those meagre means. Efficiency in project management is about producing the optimum results with the available resources, something that *Amma* has always done. Yet, I see so-called professionals, always, always, always cribbing about the inadequacy of resources. A sudden epidemic breaks out and a few of us fall sick. *Amma* almost effortlessly reorganises her schedules and creates the time to take care of us. She never complains about scarcity of time. A bunch of relatives land up unannounced and an hour later dinner is ready for them too. She neither grumbles about too much work nor cribs about additional responsibilities."

Ved's eyes were wet. So often we do not recognise the obvious. So often we understand the value of people only in their absence. Ved wanted to go to the *pooja* room and hug his mother, but didn't want to disturb the flow of his *Appa's* words. So he wiped his tears and continued to listen.

Avyakta continued, "Her approach to you is so different from her approach to parenting your brother. Temperamentally, the two of you are so different and so the approach has to be different too. That's why *Amma* always says a good mother cannot be the same mother to all her children. You should know when to stand like a rock and when to flow like the river. There are times when you have to give others their small victories and times when you have to gain the victory of the moment. In all, there are no 'no solution' moments for *Amma*. But, for most professionals there are no 'no problem' moments."

Avyakta explained, "You couldn't have asked for a better role model than *Amma* in 'Situational Leadership'. What your *Amma* could do at the micro level, with the edge you have of being a product of premium institutions, I expect you to do at the macro level. Situational Leadership is, "Let problems come from anywhere, at any time. I will find solutions for it every time." To know how to win in a situation is Situational Leadership. Instead of expecting circumstances to be customised, customising your approach to circumstances is Situational Leadership. Situational Leadership is demonstrating brilliance at the required moment. To get the best of what is there is Situational Leadership. Qualifications can give you a head start in your career, but the leader who leads by the philosophy that there are no 'no solution' situations is the leader of the future."

"Do you know Ved," Avyakta enquired, "If you put a buzzard in an eight feet square pen which is entirely open at the top, the bird, in spite of its ability to fly, will remain a prisoner! The reason is that a buzzard always begins its flight from the ground with a run of ten to twelve feet. Without space to run, as is his habit, he will not even attempt to fly, but will remain a prisoner for life in a small jail with no top. Similarly, the ordinary bat that flies around at night, a remarkably nimble creature in the air, cannot take off from a level place. If it is placed on the floor or a flat ground, all it can do is shuffle about helplessly, painfully, until it reaches some slight elevation from which it can throw itself into the air. Then, at once, it takes off in a flash. Even the bumblebee, if dropped into an open tumbler will be there until it dies, unless it is taken out. It never sees the means of escape at the top, but persists in trying to find some way out through the sides near the bottom. It will seek a way where none exists, until it completely destroys itself."

Avyakta summarised, "In many ways, there are lots of people like the buzzard, the bat and the bee. They are struggling with all their problems and frustrations, for they know not how to think according to the demands of the situation. Situational Leadership, my son, Situational Leadership... that's going to make all the difference."

Avyakta got up, hugged Ved, kissed him on the forehead and went to the master bathroom. Ved entered his bathroom. Half way through his shower, the water stopped. Soap all over him, desperate and exasperated, he was about to scream, "What do you people do in the house? Can't you keep the tank full? First day to work and..." The mantra 'Situational Leadership' lingered in the back of his mind. He re-engineered his thoughts. "How would *Amma* respond to this situation?" he enquired. Suddenly there were 'n' possibilities. His next thought was, "I couldn't have asked for a better management prophecy to begin my career. Thank you *Appa*."

Situational Leadership is,
"Let problems come from anywhere, at any time.
I will find solutions for it every time."
Instead of expecting circumstances to be
customised, customising your approach to
circumstances is Situational Leadership.
Situational Leadership is demonstrating
brilliance at the required moment.

Most and more

● ● ●

It all happens in a moment

The potency and the essence of eternity are present in every moment of life. In every seed is the promise of a forest. In every moment of life is hidden a promise that can make a man, and from that man a society can be born. History of the world is nothing but the history of significant moments. Every morning looks similar, but they are not. Every moment of life looks similar, but they are not. A zillion forces, known, unknown and unknowable, are acting upon this one moment of life. You never know which day. You never know which moment. But it will happen, when it happens, in a moment. It always happens in a moment...

•••

Holistic Life

Success is in the big things.
Happiness is in the small things.
Meditation is in nothing.
And, God is in everything.

Deepak had a big decision to make. Attending this spiritual retreat meant more than his religion to him. Ever since his first experience of this spiritual retreat, everything about his life had changed. It is here that he transcended some of his childhood phobias. It is here, for the first time, that he cried his heart out in gratitude. It is here that he developed an ear for new age music. It is here that he discovered what is it to dance in a state of trance. It is here that he had his first initiation into spirituality. It is here that he experienced his first glimpse of silence. It is here that he experienced the sanctity of a Master-Seeker relationship. This place meant everything to him.

He had a big decision to make. His child was due to be born anytime and the spiritual retreat was to begin the next day. His heart was vacillating between two equally important and defining moments. In fact, many were curious to know how Deepak would resolve this dilemma.

Though his wife could understand his feelings, she couldn't resist but ask, "What will you do if your little one does not arrive today?" Deepak replied, "Darling, my faith may be tested, but will never be forsaken. I have told you many a time that in faith even what seems wrong will eventually turn right. All things are possible in faith. My faith in the spiritual retreat is total. He will resolve it for me. I will see the arrival of my child and I will also go to the retreat so that I can arrive in my spiritual pursuit. God's delays are not god's denials."

Both of them laughed heartily, and that was it. The belly laughter gave Deepak's wife a feeling of stomach cramps. She began to feel the first traces of pain. What followed were a series of activities, and by the end of the day the melody of the baby's cries was heard. Deepak's faith caused the miracle.

The next morning, as the bus rode into the deep woods where the retreat was to take place, Deepak took the seat next to Avyakta. How often the next idea, the next thought, the next day, the next experience can change everything about your life? How often the next person you meet goes on to become one of the most significant relationships of your life? Deepak's meeting with Avyakta evolved into one such defining relationship. Everything about Deepak changed forever.

As Deepak was aware that he would have to maintain silence once Avyakta's retreat began, he chose to share his feelings with Avyakta during the bus journey. Sensitising himself to Deepak's urge to speak, Avyakta gave Deepak the needed opening, "Tell me, the latest father in town, how does it feel?"

A slight smile, moist eyes, a half-hug and then the words, "Of course, I am feeling on top of the world! I have had endless moments of success and accomplishment. I have been good at sports, at martial arts, on my career front… in fact, success is a habit for me. But nothing has touched my heart so much. While holding my baby in my hands, I experienced exactly what William Blake said,

To see a world in a grain of sand,
And a heaven in a wild flower,
Hold infinity in the palm of your hand,
And eternity in an hour.

I feel more complete now than I have ever felt before. My child is already a blessing in my life. He upheld my faith. He didn't trouble his father by creating an irresolvable dilemma. He timed his arrival. Somehow, he gives me the feeling that everything about my life is about to change, one more time."

There was a prolonged silence. When you sit with a spiritually evolved soul, even silence communicates. After some time Avyakta told Deepak, "Success is in the big things of life. Happiness is in the small things. In aspiring for the big things of life and in directing your abilities towards their fulfilment, you experience success. However, many of us are so taken up by the big things in life that we conveniently ignore the little things and the small joys of life. That's the case of a so-called successful person living a miserable life. At the other end, there are those who are so lost in the little things and the small joys of life that they don't direct their abilities towards the big things in life. That is the case of the so-called happy person living a useless - used less life. By going after the big things in life without compromising on the small things in life, man can find the otherwise elusive integration of success and happiness."

The experience of the next eight days was like life in another world. In their attempt to explain, words belittle the experience. There were processes of cleansing, purification, transcendence, bliss, love and enlightenment. It seemed as if the angels were living amongst the gods. In happiness, time shrinks. In silence, time stops. Eternity in an hour - that's what it seemed like. Eight days were over, as if they were eight hours. The end of the retreat was also the beginning of a new life for all of them.

Back to the bus and the journey back to the concrete jungle. Deepak again took his seat next to Avyakta. Again, there was a prolonged silence. Again, after some time Deepak spoke, "You told me before the retreat, 'Success is in the big things. Happiness is in the small things'. In the retreat and in the presence of the Voice that guided me in the retreat, I realised, 'Meditation is in nothing. And, God is in everything'. This retreat was your gift unto me and the way I live my life will be my gift unto you. The words with which you ended the retreat are still lingering in me... 'I not only love you but I also have the faith that my love will create you'. I won't let your love down and I know my faith will not let me down. I promise, I will lift myself and lift every life that crosses mine."

They reached the city. It felt like they were back to the future. Deepak and Avyakta parted after an elongated hug - no half measures this time. As Avyakta was leaving Deepak said, "Even after you go, you still remain with me." Avyakta remarked, "I am not a person, but a presence. With you always. Will be always.

Most and more

Wishing you most and more..." Once more, they exchanged smiles. It was a reunion between Deepak, his adult darling and the new sweetheart. Deepak's life was in full flow from one golden moment to another. How can life always be so special for special people!

A few days later, a laminated picture of his little one was found hanging on the eastern wall of the living room, with the following words inscribed.

"In your arrival I found my mantra...
Success is in the big things.
Happiness is in the small things.
Meditation is in nothing.
And, God is in everything."

**How often the next idea, the next thought,
the next day, the next experience
can change everything about your life?
How often the next person you meet
goes on to become one of the most
significant relationships in your life?**

Good name! At what cost?

Each one of you has been given a social checklist and you are expected to strictly adhere to this checklist. You will be branded selfish for your attempt to live beyond this social checklist. But, when you define, you confine. So, tear off the social checklist. Rise above the confines of social definition. Expand the definition of your life. Stand above the crowd. Live above the average man. Inspire future generations by the way you live your life. Let your life be a message to the next generation. Wake up!

"It is better to earn a bad name and live a good life, than to earn a good name and live a bad life," proclaimed Avyakta.

Most of the girls looked at each other with amusement. An elongated pause followed. The beauty of a master communicator lies not just in his ability to pack his oration with words, but also in punctuating his delivery with appropriate pauses. The mind of the receiver of the communication needs those momentary pauses for it to assimilate the idea and

Most and more

then internalise it.   Pauses in the delivery of communication are the 'think time' you build into it.   Ironically, unless it is a spiritual discourse to a spiritually aligned audience, too many pauses will create scope for a slip in their concentration. The attention of the audience will shift to something else.   Yet, very few pauses will not create the context for the message to seep into the minds of the audience. There has to be a perfect integration of pauses and words.   That's why communication is both a science and an art.

Avyakta continued, "Somehow, from the beginning, reputation has been put above character in most of your minds.   Character is 'who you are' and reputation is 'what the world thinks of you'.   You have been, time and again, asked to ensure that you earn a good name at school, a good name with your teachers, a good name in your neighbourhood, a good name with your relatives - a good name here, a good name there, a good name everywhere and every time. Such is the focus on earning a good name that the very first thought for most of you is, 'What will the world think of me if I do this or don't do it', and not 'What will I become or not become by doing this or not doing it'.   Most of you are 'other people conscious'.   {Pause} Your life is not lived through your spectacles, but through the spectacles of others.

'How should the world see me?' The answer to this question defines the context of your life. Sometimes, it isn't necessarily about earning a good name for yourself, but about earning a good name for your family, for your parents. In the entire process, most of you become puppets in the hands of the public. {Pause} You do things not because you want to do them, not because you are convinced about them, not even because you think they are right, but because they give you scope for enhancing your reputation. The potential possibility of a good name is very high. More than your desire for a good name, it is the fear of earning a bad name that drives most of your lives."

Avyakta's delivery was very fiery. Social anger was finding expression through his voice. During his oration, the passion to empower was radiating so strongly through his eyes that he didn't even blink. The strength in that voice could have come only from a heart that was weeping at this social slavery. Man has been turned against himself by making him 'other people conscious'. His main focus is no longer on 'who he is' or 'who he wishes to be', but on earning 'goodwill points' by appearing to be good in the eyes of the world. Rather than being good, it has become imperative to appear good. Avyakta was fuming. "Something within me cries…" he asserted.

Avyakta was addressing a group of 600 outgoing students in a women's college. He was convinced that we cannot awaken humanity unless we bring about a change in the mindset of the average middle-class population. When you define, you confine. The average man has been given a definition to live up to. And sure enough, he has confined himself to this social definition. A definition for 'man', a definition for 'woman', a definition for 'son', one for 'daughter' and another for 'daughter-in-law', one for 'North Indians' and another for 'South Indians', one for 'Brahmins' and another for 'Marwaris'... definitions and more definitions.

Avyakta emphasised, "Each one of you has been given a social checklist and you are expected to strictly adhere to this checklist. Your grandparents did, your parents did, so why would you rebel against it - this is the social expectation. Each of you has been parented to succumb to this social expectation. Even the slightest deviation from this social checklist will create a hullabaloo in the society. You will be branded selfish for your attempt to live beyond this social checklist. You will become a social outcast for living beyond the confines of your social definition. Hey girls, you are born in a culture where it is assumed that women are born for one singular purpose and that is to get married and be the backbone of the family. It's not about you living a life beyond tears, but about living to see others smile. There's nothing wrong in being expected to live a life that brings a smile to others, but why isn't there much respect for your tears? Girls, you have to lift yourself by yourself. Freedom is not given; it is taken. You live only once as you, and if you miss this chance, you will never have another opportunity to be yourself. Please, please do not miss yourself. Do not miss this chance. Tear off the social checklist. Rise above the confines of social definition. Pathfinders are path-breakers. Expand the definition of your life. Stand above the crowd. Live above the average man. Inspire future generations by the way you live your life. Let your life be a message to the next generation. Wake up!"

Avyakta was not talking about being a rebel without a cause. He was not talking about being irresponsible with the 'I don't care' attitude. He was not talking about being apathetic to the feelings and emotions of one's family. He was not talking about tearing off a social checklist and in turn living a characterless life. He was not talking about a 'me, mine and myself' - an absolutely selfish - life.

Avyakta explained, "Even the epitome of compassion, Lord Mahavira, professed, 'Live and let live', not 'Let live and live'. After all, if you yourself don't know how to live, then how are you going to let others live?

Most and more

The messiah of love, Jesus Christ, preached, 'Love thy neighbour as you love thyself'. Even he placed you ahead of your neighbour. Why? After all, if you don't know how to love yourself, how then will you love your neighbour? How can a beggar help others to become rich? Which slave can liberate others? How can you give the world something that you haven't first gifted to yourself? As long as you are striving for the larger good, striving for personal good doesn't make you selfish. You have the right to your fight on this planet. This earth is yours as well. This life is yours too. Use it. Don't abuse it."

Then, with a lot of compassion in his voice, Avyakta suggested, "If you do 100 things in life, do 80 things for the sake of the world, for the sake of the happiness of your family, for the sake of your parents' gratification, for the sake of social fulfilment and for the sake of your environment. Do at least 20 things in life for your own sake. Put all the aspects of your life that are of consequence, that will have a bearing on your life - such as the education you want to pursue, the career you are passionate about, the marriage you wish to settle into, the city you choose to live in - into this 20. In all these consequential aspects of life, don't give in to the confines of social definition. Write your own definition of life. Create your own checklist. Don't live by a social script. Write your own script.

In the other 80 inconsequential aspects of life, go with the world, go by the world. Even after you do 80 things for the sake of the world and only 20 things for your own sake, if the world still calls you selfish - so be it. It appears that you live in an unreasonable world. If in spite of you doing 80 things for them they are still not satisfied, then nothing is anyhow going to satisfy them. At least, satisfy yourself by doing those 20 things on your terms."

Avyakta concluded, "Let me end where I began - It is better to earn a bad name and live a good life, than to earn a good name and live a bad life. Interestingly, when you take this path, you end up living a good life and also earn a good name. Wishing each one of you most and more..."

Avyakta ended his speech. There was absolute silence in the auditorium. The girls seemed to be living by the Zen expression - speak only when you can improve upon silence. This wasn't the time to acknowledge with words. The life they would go on to live would be their acknowledgement to Avyakta. Get ready to experience the new breed, the next generation of trailblazers. Their new philosophy, "Live - 20 and let live - 80."

• • •

Being happily successful

'More' will read as 'More' any time you read it, and hence you never reach it. Hence, 'Success' is a lifelong quest. 'Enough' will read as 'Enough' any time you read it, and hence you don't have to wait another moment to experience it. Hence, 'Happiness' is just a matter of realisation. Wise are those who aspire for 'More than enough', realising that they have 'Enough' and yet go after the 'More'. This is the path to being happily successful and successfully happy.

• • •

Beyond the traffic jam

However bad the traffic jam may be, we will all eventually reach home. It may move inch by inch; it may then stop awhile; it may again move inch by inch, but eventually we will all reach home. Knowing that we will eventually reach home, we might as well not get stressed by the traffic jam. If you get stressed because of your responsibilities, you cannot respond with ability. Have faith in yourself; if you can't, then have faith in those who have faith in you. It is in moments of darkness that we discover the stars. Be a star.

The atmosphere was polluted with unhappiness. The air was suffocating. It was infected with stress and tension. You could see dis-ease in every human face that occupied the space. It seemed as if all of them were having a date with suffering.

Two carpenters were at each other's throat, both trying to prove that the other was wrong. The supervisor, with fierce expression of anger imprinted on his face, was shouting at a worker who was polishing the floor.

Most and more

The electrician was barking at his assistant for not aligning the light fitting properly. The din of human chaos and confusion was louder than all the machines in that place. It was typical of a place where everyone wanted to reach tomorrow yesterday.

Just seven days left. The invitations had already been printed and the project was to be launched in a week's time. The inauguration was slated to be a big public affair, and as with most projects, 30% of the work was done in 70% of the time, and now the remaining 70% of the work had to be done in 30% of the time. So everyone was trying to run faster than they could; everyone was trying to do more than they could. How you run the initial laps hardly counts if you don't run the final lap well. This was the final lap and this would make all the difference.

Pranav, who was in charge of Operations, was staring at the calendar wishing that he could roll it back by a week. Avyakta was on his way and was expected any moment. Pranav was waiting for Avyakta, chewing his nails; in fact, chewing even the skin around the nails, totally confused in his mind.

There was a sudden hush all over. As the commotion settled, even no noise seemed like music. There was quietude. There was a sudden calm. All of a sudden the walls seemed as though they had been coated with peace and the air felt fresh. The work was still on, but the discord was replaced with harmony. From nowhere smiles had bloomed on so many faces. Their solution finder had just arrived. Avyakta was just getting out of the car. For some reason in Avyakta's presence, no one exhales problems; everyone inhales solutions.

Avyakta walked in with dishevelled hair, wearing a T-Shirt and jeans, sandals, hardly the attire for someone who is looked up to as a mentor by so many people, but that's Avyakta. You see, when you have a personality you do not have to wear a personality. Avyakta greeted everyone, from the security guard to the mason and the cleaner, even before they could open their mouth. Within moments, the place was transformed to one where dignity reigned supreme, irrespective of who they were and what they were doing.

A learned man once said, "Wherever you go you will be miserable, because you are still there." The converse was true with Avyakta. Wherever he went there was happiness, because he was there.

As he crossed the supervisor whose face revealed enormous stress, Avyakta just threw his arms around him and said, "Happy morning! I want everyone who is associated with this project to feel on 'Top of the World', and not as if, there is a 'World on their Top'. What cannot be achieved with happiness can never be achieved out of unhappiness. If you get stressed because of your responsibilities, you cannot respond with ability. Have faith in yourself; if you can't, then have faith in those who have faith in you. I have faith in you. Wash your face with cold water. Take a few deep breaths. Relax. Smile. Inhale solutions. The project will take off as per schedule. I see all green lights."

How often people process the problems of the coming year, the coming month and the coming week, and fail to do anything about what could have been done that day? The word 'problem' had been banned from Avyakta's vocabulary. He would often say, "Driving the car through the traffic without the steering wheel is, of course, a problem; but, with the steering wheel, it is just a challenge? Compared to the infinite human potential each one of us is bestowed with, can any situation about life be termed a problem?" What is the point in overburdening ourselves with tomorrow's challenges today? After all, what can be done tomorrow can be done only tomorrow! The secret of unburdening is to focus on getting your 'today' right. Never make your today the enemy of your tomorrow. Anything done out of unhappiness will only bring multiplied unhappiness.

As Avyakta finished with the supervisor, he turned towards Pranav, who was attempting to smile at Avyakta, but then the body never lies. The stress he was under was very evident; his smile was like flowers placed on a dead body. Pranav had a block between his two ears, and when that happens, what you hear doesn't go inside, but instead on all sides. With most of our challenges, the actual challenge is not out there in the world but between our two ears. Some people go out looking for trouble, and sure enough, they find it. Others never trouble the trouble until trouble troubles them. The hammer that shatters glass forges steel. So, what troubles and challenges do to you depends on who you are and how you see them. Two men looked through the prison bars. One saw the mud and the other saw the stars. The tests of life are to make us, not break us. All troubles eventually end. So why be troubled by troubles?

In a corner, a temporary arrangement had been made with a rented table and four chairs to conduct all the discussions. Just ten feet away, a carpenter was at work making a deafening noise with his tools. Pranav had already reached for his chair. As he went past the carpenter, Avyakta beamed a beautiful smile and nodded his head at the carpenter. The carpenter immediately stopped his work, reciprocated the smile and left the place saying he would return in 15 minutes.

Most and more

How true that a simple gesture from a heart overflowing with love and happiness can communicate more than all the words that come from the lips! Pranav was flipping through his checklist restlessly tossing his attention from one page to another like a butterfly, unsure about which flower to sit on.

Avyakta patted Pranav's head in a friendly manner and took a chair. Impetuously Pranav started, "Regarding the reception area..." Avyakta intervened and said assertively, "Pranav I want to speak to you first. I will listen to you later. Shall I?" Pranav drew back the papers, straightened his back and nodded.

Avyakta continued, "I do not want any success in my organisation that comes at the cost of happiness. Do you realise that the energy you thus exude, out of your unhappiness, has such a harmful effect that you are contaminating yourself as well as those around you? We are just getting a project ready, not fighting a war. I can see worries and tension written across everyone's face. Why don't they realise that the negative vibrations they create are going to act as the greatest impediment to the success of the project? We are here to clear the mess, not create the mess. If you are centred and happy, then going through tough times is not tough. Let me repeat, what cannot be achieved through happiness can never be achieved through unhappiness. Let everything come and go... not the undercurrent of happiness. A happy heart radiates those positive vibrations that have the power to bring divinity to your doorstep. I want an organisation that is happily successful."

There was earnestness on Pranav's face. He was willing to change his ways and progress, rather than stick to his own ways and fail. Even if he could not be Avyakta, he certainly wanted to live the Avyakta's way. His eyes communicated, "I want to be that heart which is always centred on happiness and love, but how?"

Avyakta continued, "Without getting things within you right, nothing outside will become right. So constantly ask yourself, 'Am I at ease with this moment?' Like the beating of your heart, like your breathing, let this be an incessant lingering, 'Am I at ease with this moment?' If you aren't, then you don't have to change 'what' you are doing; it is sufficient to change 'how' you are doing it. When any moment puts you at dis-ease, first *accept what is* and then follow it up with a prudent choice: *change it if it can be changed,* else *remove yourself from it.*"

"Got it Pranav?" asked Avyakta. As he was speaking, Pranav closed the file, which contained all the papers. Avyakta then said, "Now let us discuss what you want to discuss with me. I am ready to listen. Shoot."

Most and more

Pranav smiled in return, cast a glance at his watch and said, "Happy afternoon, Chief! Nothing to discuss. I can take care. In fact, I want to take care. The project will start on time. Consider it done. Chief, you can concentrate on all other arrangements. This project, remove yourself from it; I mean from the perspective of work. I will happily get everything done. Now that I understand that a happy heart radiates those positive vibrations that have the power to bring divinity to your doorstep, I will keep expecting you at my doorstep too often."

Avyakta got up, hugged Pranav and added, "It is in moments of darkness that we discover the stars. Here you have your opportunity. Above everything that I have said, remember this," and Avyakta added, "However bad the traffic jam may be, we will all eventually reach home. It may move inch by inch; it may then stop awhile; it may again move inch by inch, but eventually we will all reach home. Knowing that we will eventually reach home, we might as well not get stressed by the traffic jam. Catch you beyond the traffic jam, I mean, at the inaugural function." Pranav hugged Avyakta once again before he left.

A week later, thousands of people attended the inaugural function. As the ribbon was cut to a thunderous applause, Avyakta and Pranav winked at each other with a naughty smile. This is not something that you associate with someone of Avyakta's stature, but then, that's Avyakta, everything with a bit of naughtiness. Pranav offered a neatly wrapped gift to Avyakta, and with a surprised expression, Avyakta too extended a wrapped gift to Pranav. Avyakta opened his gift with gentle grace, as if he were handling an infant, and found a specially made tabletop display with the words, "However bad the traffic jam may be, we will all eventually reach home." As Pranav ripped open his gift, he was pleasantly surprised to see that even his gift was a specially made tabletop display with the words, "It is in moments of darkness that we discover the stars. Wishing you most and more..."

Pranav commented, "Is it, chief, that fools think alike?" Avyakta nodded his head disapprovingly and said, "Wise men seldom differ."

Some people never change... I'm speaking about Avyakta.

**Without getting things within you right,
nothing outside will become right.
So ask yourself, 'Am I at ease with this moment?'
If you aren't, then you don't have to change
'what' you are doing; it is sufficient to change
'how' you are doing it.**

●●●

Use it or lose it

Unused money devalues. Unused talent diminishes. Unused potential decays. Unused machinery disintegrates. Unused time dies. Unused knowledge becomes a burden. What isn't used is abused. The tragedy of life isn't the ultimate death, but the resources that die within you when you are still alive. Use it, or you will lose it.

●●●

Expectation Management

You cannot stand under a mango tree and expect oranges. What is even more foolish is blaming the mango tree for not fulfilling your expectations. So, either change your expectations according to the tree or find a tree that matches your expectations. Turn all the expectations you have from the world unto yourself. That's the way to peaceful progress in life.

"I don't think I have a future in this organisation. I am just dragging myself to work every morning. I have lost the motivation to put in those long hours at work. If I continue to work in this place, I will slip into a low performing or non-performing zone. It's frustrating. I joined the organisation with great expectations, and this is where I find myself six months later! I don't know why, except my first job which was with you, I have never been lucky to find the right work environment," vented Sanjay to Avyakta.

Satisfied needs don't motivate man. The West envies the spiritual roots of the East and the East desires the materialism of the West. We always want to trade places. "If only I had your experience," uttered the youth. "If only I had your age," retorted the one with experience. In every person's career, there are times when earning takes precedence over learning, and times when learning takes priority over earning. However, there is no rationale behind the impulses of the heart. What satisfies the heart, what leaves it dissatisfied, why it gets transfixed, why it moves on, why it chooses to drop what it chooses to drop... there is no reasoning behind it. After all, man is not a creature of logic, but a creature of emotions. Therein lies the uniqueness of this creation and also the beauty of life. Even man knows not what is coming from himself.

It was a dream come true for any management graduate to be mentored by Avyakta. After completing his MBA, Sanjay joined Avyakta's consulting firm as a management trainee. Avyakta professionally mentored him for two years. Lured by the position he was offered in an MNC, he made the move. In the next four years, he changed five jobs. A student can give up on a teacher, but a teacher must not give up on a student, and if he does, it only means that though teaching may be his profession, he does not have the heart of a teacher. A trifle perturbed by the instability of Sanjay's career, Avyakta called him over for a discussion. Nothing is more disheartening than seeing someone who showed enormous promise in the beginning become an also-ran. Avyakta was concerned.

No doubt, Sanjay had incomparable talent; he had a mind that could always think the unthought. Yet, Sanjay had this limitation - nothing and nobody satisfied him. He was a man perpetually disturbed. Nothing excited him for too long. Everything and everybody became boring after some time. He did look up to Avyakta but he couldn't even stand Avyakta beyond two years. The good news in this otherwise bad story is that Sanjay wasn't married yet. God bless the woman already marked for Sanjay!

Avyakta allowed Sanjay to pour out his frustration and empty his mind. You listen best when you have nothing more to say. An unburdened mind is a receptive mind. Sanjay's eyes confirmed that he was ready to absorb, and he knew that something within him needed correction. He realised that an organisation not being compatible with his personal needs and necessities does not make the organisation wrong. It's an issue of the chemistry not working, not a matter of who is right and what is wrong. He was ready to change. Who other than Avyakta could reflect Sanjay to Sanjay and also suggest corrections?

Avyakta said, "You cannot stand under a mango tree and expect oranges. What is even more foolish is blaming the mango tree for not fulfilling your expectations. So, either change your expectations according to the tree or find a tree that matches your expectations. Don't continue to stand under a mango tree feeling frustrated that you are not getting oranges and keep accusing the mango tree for it. Don't be stupid."

Avyakta continued, "This isn't the case with you alone; it seems to be the predicament of mankind. In employer-employee relationships, in customer-vendor relationships, in parent-child relationships, in man-woman relationships, man's quandary seems to be 'mismanaged expectations'. I don't want to sound too much like Buddha by asking you to drop your expectations, but I want to take the pragmatic approach by telling you to manage your expectations better."

"First and foremost of all," Avyakta said, "realise that a mango tree is a mango tree. It was meant to be a mango tree; it will remain a mango tree, and from it you can get only mangoes. Irrespective of your expectations, it will produce only mangoes. People are what they are. An organisation is what it is. Life is what life is. You expect people to be other than what they are and get frustrated with them. You expect an organisation to be other than what it is and get frustrated with it. Your expectation for oranges from a mango tree not being fulfilled isn't the fault of the mango tree. This is what I call mismanaged expectations. If you think no organisation is giving you the right work environment, then why don't you start an organisation of your own and run it on your terms. Why not create the environment you want? This is what I mean when I say find a tree that matches your expectations; grow your own tree."

"Sanjay, if you want peaceful progress in life, follow these guidelines," said Avyakta, "One, define your expectations. More often than not, we aren't sure ourselves as to what we expect. We order an item from the menu card and seeing what the person on the adjacent table is eating we think 'maybe I should have ordered that'. So, first stop being such a confused person, lest you confuse the world around you. Two, clarify your expectations explicitly. So often, others don't even know what you are expecting from them; then how can they fulfil it for you? Life is already complex. Let us not complicate it further. Please simplify life for others by clarifying your expectations clearly and explicitly. Three, in case your expectations are not fulfilled, check if you are expecting oranges from a mango tree. If you find you are only expecting mangoes from a mango tree, then keep communicating long enough; keep clarifying your expectations patiently. Sure enough, patience and perseverance will eventually bear fruit. If this isn't the case, for instance, in key relationships where you cannot change the tree, learn to accept the mango tree as a mango tree and change your expectations according to it. It will leave you in peace. For your own sake, develop a taste for mangoes. In cases like organisations, where change is possible, find a tree according to your expectations. Rather than trying to change the world, change what is within your control, which is your own self. This will give you progress."

Finally, with a lot of assertiveness, Avyakta added, "Above all, Sanjay, the greatest learning in expectation management is: 'Turn all the expectations you have from the world unto yourself'. When expectations are directed towards the world, your peace and progress is at the mercy of the world. Turn them onto yourself, and you will be in control of your life. That's why I am telling you, need be, grow your own tree. Need be, build your own personal world within this physical world, and that will be your world on your terms."

Avyakta hugged Sanjay and whispered in his ears, "How I wish all of us were taught this very early in life: 'Neither will all your expectations be fulfilled, nor will all your expectations remain unfulfilled'. Often, He will upset your plans in order to execute His plans for you. You go after oranges and I'll go after mangoes, remembering, it is not my will, but it is Thy will that will be done. Wishing you most and more... And, let this be the beginning of peaceful progress in your life."

While working with him, Sanjay had heard Avyakta say so many times, "Some speeches are born out of certain lives. And, certain lives are born out of certain speeches." Sanjay knew in the heart of his hearts that every time he had the blessing of listening to Avykta, something about his life changed forever... his life was reborn.

First, define your expectations. More often than not, we aren't sure ourselves as to what we expect. Then, clarify your expectations explicitly. So often, others don't even know what you are expecting from them; then how can they fulfil it for you? Three, in case your expectations are not fulfilled, rather than trying to change the world, change what is within your control, which is your own self. This will give you progress. How I wish all of us were taught this very early in life: 'Neither will all your expectations be fulfilled, nor will all your expectations remain unfulfilled'.

Most and more

• • •

Hallmark of greatness

Consistency is the hallmark of greatness. Anyone can perform an occasional act of greatness. Truly great are those who can consistently perform acts of greatness. You will not be remembered for what you do or did once in a way, but for what you do and did all the time.

•••

To lead the leader

The lawyer and the judge cannot be the same. You need someone outside of you to have an objective view of what you do and what you don't. A coach is like the third eye. A small difference can be the defining criteria between a good player and a great player, and that's where the coach comes in.

A desire entertained and not fulfilled becomes an incomplete cycle. Every incomplete cycle, in some way, keeps nagging you from within. There is this constant sense of incompleteness. Truly, it is a sort of psychological irritation. Either release the desire, or fulfil it. Don't leave it hanging. Every incomplete cycle saps you of your energy, leaving you drained and fatigued. That's why it isn't the day you worked a lot that tires you, but the day when many things remained incomplete that tires you.

Swimming was Avyakta's incomplete cycle. He always wanted to learn to swim, but it was one of those things that didn't happen for Avyakta. When he had the time he didn't have the money, and when he had the money he didn't have the time. When he found a way to enjoy the best of both - time and money, his life became too purposeful for him to pursue individual aspirations. But then, an incomplete cycle is an incomplete cycle. The mind knows the reasons; the heart cares not. "There are people who make things happen, there are people who watch things happen, and there are people who wonder what happened. To be successful, you need to be a person who makes things happen," said James A. Lovell, and it is not without a reason that Avyakta was successful.

Avyakta epitomised the words of Henry David Thoreau: "If one advances confidently in the direction of his dreams, and endeavours to live the life which he has imagined, he will meet with success unexpected in common hours." He didn't want to carry the load of this incomplete cycle, when something could actually be done about it. So, Avyakta enrolled himself for a swimming class, and Vel became his personal coach. Avyakta had told others so many times, "Keep the student within you alive," and now it was his turn to practice it. When you seek to know, it isn't the time to show what you know. Here was Avyakta, a student once again after several decades, practicing the flutter kick, and not getting it right. After every spell of kicking, this otherwise successful man would look at his coach with longing in his eyes, only to hear comments like, "The feet are down or the knees are bent, the left leg is not moving properly, etc..."

There was visible joy on Avyakta's face when he was able to move from one end of the pool to the other the first time, still doing flutter kick. Success is role dependent. Success is task dependent. When a Fortune 500 CEO makes coffee for the first time, that's a moment of success for him - all the more so if it tastes good. When a speaker sings in public for the first time or when a singer speaks in public for the first time, that's a moment of success. So what if Avyakta has seen it all - the twists and turns of the script of life... in the swimming pool, he was still a novice. Vel, the coach, then initiated Avyakta into hand movements and then added breathing techniques to it. After every lap, convinced it was a fabulous attempt, Avyakta would look in the direction of his coach. Typical of Vel, he would remark, "Your elbow is not rising, your legs are going down when you take a breath, or don't hold the body so tight, just relax, etc..." So what if so many awards and accolades have already filled the shelves in Avyakta's house, here he was craving to hear one 'Good job' from his swimming coach, which was still eluding him.

As Avyakta was walking towards the parking lot after his swimming session one day, a set of thoughts flashed through his mind. "My coach wants me to get a 100. His feedbacks on my shortcomings come from his standpoint that I am short of 100. I am evaluating my current performance vis-à-vis my previous performance. I am elated because I feel I have moved from 61 to 64, and today I feel I have reached 65. I am celebrating my progress. My coach is striving for my perfection. If he too becomes content and celebrates my progress, if he too becomes ecstatic with my 65, then the loss will be mine. While the player can motivate himself on the grounds of his progress, he certainly needs a coach who is dissatisfied with anything that's less than 100. A coach who will never settle for anything less than 100 is truly a boon for a player."

Avyakta grew in respect for Vel. Avyakta understood the context from which a coach comes. Vel's dissatisfaction became Avyakta's inspiration. Avyakta began to give his very best and that little more every time he came back to the pool. Every taste of success propels you to seek more success, because success breeds success. Avyakta kept growing - 68, 72, 77... but Vel wasn't a man who would settle for anything less.

Avyakta's contemplations on the role of a coach deepened. The lawyer and the judge cannot be the same. You need someone outside of you to have an objective view of what you do and what you don't. He was convinced that a coach is like the third eye. In spite of all the technology, the player cannot watch his own game objectively. Sometimes, a little fine-tuning - a bending of the knee, the racket angle, the shoulder positioning, tilt of the head - a small difference can be the defining criteria between a good player and a great player, and that's where the coach comes in.

Avyakta grew in contemplation. Why an auditor? Why an auditor for an auditing firm? Why examiners? Why inspection of those very examiners? Why a board of directors? Why do even the greatest of champions have a coach? How can a coach add value to a world champion? The answer to all the questions led Avyakta to the same answer - someone outside of you should observe you and reveal you to yourself. Why?

When you have lived next to a busy road for too long, you will no more hear traffic sounds. Even for the most objective of people, when they have lived with certain objectives for too long, their very objectives becomes subjective. We become prejudiced about anything that we are greatly attached to. Then there is no more a question of objectivity. This is where the third eye comes in. This is where an observer's point of view becomes so critical. This is where someone who can evaluate you on a 100, and show you where you are falling short, can make all the difference.

The most essential quality of a good coach is not that he has to be better than you, but he should be a great observer and a reader of you. He may not be able to achieve what you may be able to achieve, but his achievement lies in making you an achiever. After all, I don't have to be a bull in order to train a bull; I just need to know how to train one.

Avyakta visualised a king's court with all the ministers; the traditional version of a boardroom. The king, with the aid of his ministers, would administer the kingdom. The court has a *Raja-Guru* - a Royal Preceptor. While the king takes care of the kingdom, the *Raja-Guru* takes care of the king. The kingdom turns to the king and the king turns to the *Raja-Guru*.

Avyakta realised the need for a *Raja-Guru*, for a life-coach in his life. He was convinced that it will make all the difference. "Who will be my third eye?" he wondered.

For the while, he was again in the swimming pool, taking his first lessons on backstroke. One of the secrets of youthfulness is to keep the student within you always alive... And, it is not without a reason that Avyakta is Avyakta.

A good coach need not be better than you, but he should be a great observer of you.
I don't have to be a bull in order to train a bull.
I just need to know how to train one.

● ● ●

To leave a legacy

Man is the only creation capable of leaving a legacy and to live beyond his lifetime. It is not just a possibility, but also a responsibility for leaders to leave a legacy by creating more leaders.

"Even when I am inside, I should feel I am outside." This was Avyakta's instruction to his architects, while handing over the project of designing his office. The architects designed and executed 'a one of its kind' office by incorporating all the five elements of nature, namely fire, water, earth, air and space. All over the world, places most visited by humans are those that are aligned to these five elements. Even the worktops and seating were sculpted out of natural stones. There was hardly any artificial touch in that office. Even the doors and windowpanes were made of raw, unfinished wood. The credit to the architects lay in the fact that their presence could be felt in every inch, and yet nothing was too obvious. It was sublime. Even when I am inside, I should feel I am outside - the vision was now a reality.

Right outside Avyakta's office, there was a granite erection obstructing the entrance. It was by design.

It was deliberately placed to make all those who visited Avyakta read the words engraved on it. Engraved on it were the words of the illustrious George Bernard Shaw. These words were very close to Avyakta's heart. In fact, Avyakta's organisational logo was designed from these words.

The Splendid Torch - George Bernard Shaw

"This is the true joy in life, the being used for
a purpose recognised by yourself as a mighty one.
I am of the opinion that my life belongs to the whole
community, and as long as I live it is my privilege
to do for it whatever I can. I want to be thoroughly
used up when I die, for the harder I work the more
I live. I rejoice in life for its own sake. Life is no
'brief candle' for me. It is a sort of splendid torch
which I have got hold of for the moment, and I want
to make it burn as brightly as possible before
handing it on to future generations."

It was an everyday ritual for Avyakta to stand before the granite inscription, and read the words as if he were taking an oath, and only then begin his work. The first meeting of the day was slated with the architects. It was supposed to be a meeting for Avyakta to thank his architects and for the architects to express their gratitude for the experience gained by working with Avyakta. The architects turned up on time; this is a culture Avyakta had developed around him - punctuality. Mutual expressions of gratitude, appreciation and observations were shared.

One of the architects commented, "I know these words speak about creating and leaving a legacy. I do understand that the need to leave a legacy is our spiritual need. Yet, the devotion I see in you for these words is truly amazing."

Avyakta smiled and explained, "We enjoy what we accumulate in a lifetime, but the world enjoys what we create and leave behind. Of all the creations man alone is aware of death. Man alone knows his life has a limited lifespan. The context of death puts a premium on life. The background of death demands a purpose and meaning from one's life. I want it to be recorded that I lived. I don't want to be a statistical entity, whose arrival, survival and departure, all remained unnoticed by the world. What I do is not for personal gain alone; it is my way of acknowledging that when God breathed in my nostrils and gave me life, He intended for me to use it well."

There was a prolonged silence. The architect who had made the observation gulped some water. Avyakta added, "When I die the world will inscribe on my tombstone the year of my birth and the year of my death separated by a dash (1965 - 20??). That dash is my life. What I did, how I lived, the lives I touched, what I created, the legacy I leave behind... they all represent that dash. My purpose in life is to make that dash as meaningful and as memorable as possible. The best of legacies are the by-products of a life well lived. I will die, but the legacy I create and leave behind shall never die."

Avyakta walked over to the side of the architect and throwing his arm around the architect's shoulders he continued, "When I live just for my today, I feel nice - a life of daily wages. When I live for my tomorrow, I feel good - the category of monthly salaries. It is only when I live for what I can create for generations to come that I feel great. When the focus is to keep the torch burning and to pass it on to the generations to come, then the motivation levels are truly celestial."

Just then they were served bowls of fruit salad. Picking up a piece of apple by the fork and holding it up, as if it was a visual aid, Avyakta said, "We are enjoying the legacy created by someone. We didn't plant the apple seed, nor did we nurture the apple tree; but we are enjoying the fruits of someone else's labour. From timeless wisdom to modern technology, everything that we enjoy and benefit is someone else's legacy. If we have the right to enjoy these legacies, then we also have the responsibility to create and leave behind a legacy. There are no 'Rights' without responsibilities. It is up to us to live up to the legacy that was left for us, and to leave a legacy for those who will come after us."

There was contemplative silence, but the process of emptying the fruits from the bowls continued. Avyakta said, "The minimum I can do is to plant some trees and nurture them, so that the future generations can enjoy the fruits and bask in the shade of that tree. Every man has the responsibility to ask this question, 'What can I add to this world that did not exist when I was born?' It could be writing a book, creating breakthrough systems, innovating a new business model, giving birth to a new culture - a new mindset, transforming the life of a village, educating the masses... it could be transforming the life of a village, it could be educating the masses... it could be anything. As an architect you should create a structure that will outlive your lifetime and also be treasured by generations to come. Have you realised that the icon of most cities and countries is an architectural creation? So, creating something iconic will be the legacy you can create."

"As a person working with the minds of people," Avyakta said, "I also want to achieve something else. The secret of legendary success is in successive greatness.

Most and more

Successive greatness and continuity of leadership has been the sole secret of all legendary results, whether political, spiritual, industrial or arts. Study the history of any legendary success and you will discover successive greatness. So, one of the most important legacies every leader is responsible for creating is to build more leaders, not mere followers. In working with the minds of people, we can enable them to continue from where we left. Our ends can be their beginning. It is only through this continuity that humanity will remain an evolving consciousness. God created me to create. God has given me most and more, and now it is my responsibility to give back to the world most and more... I will create a legacy. When I leave, I will leave behind a legacy."

Finally the architects got up to leave, feeling a little restless. And won't they be, for this thought will continue to haunt them: "What can I create that will outlive my lifetime?" After the meeting, Avyakta was seen planting a banyan sapling in the north-eastern corner of his office.

Man alone can immortalise himself by what he creates and leaves behind. Much after you and I are physically gone, you and I can continue to live spiritually through the legacy we create and leave behind. In that sense, you and I shall never die.

• • •

When I reached there,
there was no there

We are not born only to die, but we are also born to serve. Not for this, and not for that... not to book your place in heaven, nor to win a coveted award that can be bestowed upon you - but for the sheer joy of being useful - after all, the only other choice is to be useless - used less.

Was he feeling lonely or did he want to be alone? Loneliness is a consequence. You want people, but no one is around. Aloneness is a choice. People want to be with you, but you don't want anyone around. He is a man who makes choices. He must have wanted to be alone. He was driving alone and driving aimlessly. He was going nowhere. Just flowing, like the river beside the road.

The road and the river were running parallel for quite a distance. He stopped his car. There was nothing special about that spot. From its origin to the point where it merges with the ocean, the river runs several hundred kilometres. Why this spot?

Most and more

If only everything about life can be explained!! That's why the mystics refer to life as purposeless significance - significant, but there isn't necessarily a purpose behind everything. Life is best lived when you don't try to demystify everything about life.

There must have been a call from that space. The heart often hears such calls that the mind never comprehends. Avyakta ambled across to the rocky bank of the river. He sat on a rock and kept staring at the flowing river. How often the subject feels so connected to the object that the subject actually becomes the object. Avyakta lost himself to the river.

He wondered, "It seems as though the river is running bordered by the two banks. Yet, beneath the river the two banks are actually connected. Deep inside, there are no two banks - just one continuous flow appearing to be separated at the surface by the flowing river. Yet, the banks derive their identity from the river. On the banks of the Ganges and on the banks of Indus they say... yet, all mud and all sand is just one continuous flow."

Nodding his head, as if he was endorsing his own thoughts, Avyakta thought, "Spiritually, the spark of life that enlivens me and the spark of life that enlivens all beings is one and the same. Spiritually, all of us are connected like the banks of the river. Deep inside, there is no separation. Yet, physically I am unique and I am the only one of my kind. I am completely different from every other being in the world, in every sense. Like the Ganges and the Indus follow their own paths and have their own identities."

"Eureka!" Avyakta thought, "Now I know why I want the whole world with me sometimes and why I don't want anyone at other times. Whenever the spiritual need within me expresses itself, because all beings and I are one and the same, I feel like being with all. The need for connectivity manifests itself and I wish to be part of a crowd, a fraternity, and an association. I want to be the 'we'! However, whenever the physicality of my being takes over, the physical needs of individuality take over and I crave for identity - I want to be different from others. I want to be above others. I want to be ahead of others. I want to be the 'I'."

Avyakta concluded that thought flow, "So, I will remain caught between these paradoxical needs - the spiritual need for connectivity and hence the desire to relate with all, and the physical need for individuality and hence the need for personal identity. So, sometime I will complement others and complete them. At other times I will compete with them and make them feel incomplete. When I have this I will want that, and when I have that I will want this. Life is thus designed by the Wisdom above so that I can flow between these two seemingly different needs, though deep inside they are two sides of the same coin."

The evening was fading away. Avyakta returned to his car. He didn't start the ignition. His mind was thinking hard. His mind was racing against itself in contemplation. Eureka again! He thought, "Similarly, the geometry of life is designed to keep us at the point of maximum tension between certainty and uncertainty, order and chaos. There is an order to everything in Existence. And when this orderliness expresses itself through man, he needs certainty. He wants to be sure, confident, clear, convinced, predictable, safe, and secure. However, there is also chaotic randomness behind this order, which is why nothing repeats itself in Existence. And when this randomness expresses itself through man, he seeks uncertainty. He seeks adventure, risk, amusement, suspense, exploration, freshness and newness. Once again, man is caught between another pair of paradoxical needs - the need for certainty and the need for uncertainty. Again, life is thus designed by Existential wisdom so that man can find order through certainty and growth through uncertainty, both of which man needs - order and growth - for his existence."

"Now I understand the cycle of life," Avyakta thought to himself, "Everything is in current. Everything is in one continuous flow. Life is from this to that and then from that to this. The water evaporates and goes up only to come down. We learn to read and then read to learn. Every child becomes the father of man. From the seed a tree, from the tree a fruit, and from the fruit again a seed. Now I know why the earth is round! Now I understand why the planets orbit in revolution. Now I understand recycling. Now I understand Existence. Now I can comprehend the evolution and the revolutions behind the evolution."

Avyakta smiled again and gently said, "Here goes the next pair of paradoxical needs - the need to 'have' and the need to 'give'. When the need to 'have' expresses itself, man desires to possess - the selfishness within him gains expression. When the need to 'give' expresses itself, man desires to share - the unselfishness within him finds expression. After all, I can give only what I have. So the need to have always precedes the need to give. The need to possess precedes the need to share. Every selfish man will be unselfish at some time to somebody on some occasion."

So often Avyakta has wondered, "No matter how much we achieve, there is a point at which all of us will once again feel like a failure. You run the race of life in laps to discover that every finishing line is also the starting line. You run and run only to get back to where you started. As the success graph of life keeps soaring, you only realise, year after year that the closing balance once again becomes the opening balance, and you start all over again. The axis is always reset and you find yourself at '0, 0' on the graph of life, no matter how much you grow or how much you achieve. All these eventually leave you with the question - 'Is this all worth it?' What then is the purpose of life?"

Avyakta would no more ask these questions. Today he had found his answers. From the driver's seat he glanced at the river one more time and said to himself, "Flow, flow like the river. Born choicelessly, flow gleefully and merge with the ocean. In between, in the natural course of your flow, be as useful as you can be to one and all. Like the river that dances between the two banks, caught between the six innate paradoxical needs with which man is designed - connectivity and individuality, certainty and uncertainty, to 'have' and to 'give' - keep growing, keep giving and keep living. Not necessarily serving a purpose, but ensuring you add significance to everything and everybody you meet on the way. We are not born only to die, but we are also born to serve. Not for this, and not for that... not to book your place in heaven, nor to win a coveted award that can be bestowed upon you - but, for the sheer joy of being useful - after all, the only other choice is to be useless - used less."

Whether you are useful or useless, the six feet beneath is reserved for all of us. "After the game, the king and the pawn go into the same box," goes the Italian saying. True, but why be a pawn, when you can be the king? As the king, you can serve so many and be useful to so many. Remember, "Service to humanity is the rent we pay for living on this planet." What we do for ourselves will die with us; what we do for others and for the world will be left behind and will remain immortal.

Avyakta's mind concluded, "There is no there to reach. No end. No beginning. Just a flow... a useful perennial flow."

No matter how much we achieve, there is a point at which all of us will once again feel like a failure. You run the race of life in laps to discover that every finishing line is also the starting line. You only realise, year after year that the closing balance once again becomes the opening balance, and you start all over again.

Most and more

● ● ●

Life is a game

In a world of progress, there is no Midas touch. There is no such person as 'he got it right all the time'. Nobody succeeds all the time. Nobody is destined to remain a failure either. Neither failure is final nor success is permanent. Today's success and today's failures are just another step in the long journey of life. Life is a game. If you play this game long enough, you will make it. Don't quit midway. Play. Play to the end. Play it long enough. Eventually, you will cross the finishing line.

My life is my Prayer

While all the resources of my life are God's gift unto me, the work I create out of all these resources is actually my creation. True, the flowers, the fruits and the air that I have to articulate to pray in words are all His. Even this very me is only His. But the work I create out of all these resources is my creation. If all the work I do becomes my offering unto my God, then my very life becomes a prayer unto Him.

Everything was going right with his life. Everything! There was health, wealth, love, bliss... he was living life to the hilt. In fact, his response to "How are you?" had become "Flowing with life."

Avyakta's life was completely spiritually aligned. His prayers were never a petition to his Lord. He never asked for more or asked his god to alter something about his life. He would often say, "I don't tell my god what He should be doing or what He should not be doing. Without god, I cannot. Without me, god will not. Doing the best is my job, and doing the rest is

His job. Of course, if I don't do my best, then He will just take rest."

However, that evening he decided to visit a temple. With teary eyes, standing in front of the altar of his god, Avyakta's thought flow was: "You have given me everything and I want to give you something in return. I thought I would offer you flowers, but these flowers are already yours. Whose flowers do I offer to whom? I thought I would offer you fruits, but these fruits too are yours. Oh Lord, you have given me everything and I want to give you something in return, but everything is already yours. Why have you rendered me so helpless that I have nothing to give you? I thought I would at least pray to you in words, but even the very air that I articulate is yours. You have given me everything my Lord, but I have nothing to give you, in return. In a state of complete gratitude and helplessness, where I have nothing to offer to you, I drop this body of mine at your feet." Saying so, Avyakta prostrated before the altar of his God.

With tears of overwhelming gratitude still streaming down his face, he sat in silence in an isolated corner of the temple. The senses had withdrawn themselves and Avyakta seemed to be in a state of trance, but he was not. His heart was in a state of communion, and his mind was communicating with itself.

He was contemplating in his silent chambers. There was a parade of thoughts, and yet there was profound clarity in the flow of those thoughts. Avyakta was still in control of his thoughts. He knew what he was thinking.

Avyakta was thinking: "Coordinating resources in a certain order to serve a specific function is called work. Bringing the fingers together in a certain order to hold a pen and then moving the hand in a certain order is writing. Directing the mind in a certain order is thinking. Mobilising the tongue in a certain order is speech. Coordinating the body, mind and emotions in a certain order is action. Coordinating action to serve a defined objective is work. So, work is effective management of resources in a certain order to achieve a specific, functional objective."

Avyakta said to himself, "While all the resources of my life are God's gift unto me, the work I create out of all these resources is actually my creation. True, the flowers, the fruits and the air that I have to articulate to pray in words are all His. Even this very me is only His. But the work I create out of all these resources is my creation."

By then, the tears had dried on his cheeks. He gently opened his eyes and returned to the altar of his god. He prayed, "Oh Lord, all the work I do is my creation.

Though it is all out of your resources, it is still my creation. From now on, I shall no more pray to you in words, nor perform any rituals. I will not offer you flowers or fruits. However, all the work I do from now on will be my offering unto you. Lord, because I offer you nothing but the best, all the work I do from now on will be nothing but the best. Everything I have in my life is your gift unto me. My Lord, everything I will do in my life will be my gift, my offering, my expression of gratitude unto you."

Avyakta then gently closed his eyes and added, "If all the work I do is my offering unto you, then my very life becomes a prayer unto you. My life will be my prayer, my Lord."

An oft-repeated phrase in history is, "And one day, everything changed." In that sense, it was a historic day for Avyakta. Everything about his life changed on that day, in those few minutes.

The disciple asked the Master, "Now that you are enlightened, what do you do in life?" The Master replied, "I draw water from the well and chop wood." The disciple again asked, "Before you got enlightened, what were you doing?" The Master replied again, "I used to draw water from the well and chop wood." Puzzled, the disciple commented, "There seems to be no difference in your life, before and after enlightenment." The Master smiled and added, "There has been no change in my actions, but the quality with which I perform my actions has completely changed."

Right! In some ways, nothing of Avyakta's life changed. But in another way, everything about his life had changed. The quality with which he performed his actions, and as a result, the quality with which he lived his life, everything had changed.

Some people meditate in life. For some, life itself is meditation. Some people pray in life. For Avyakta, his very life has become his prayer.

Oh my Lord,
You have given me everything
and I want to give you something in return.
I thought I would offer you flowers,
but these flowers are already yours.
Whose flowers do I offer to whom?
I thought I would at least pray to you in words, but
even the very air that I articulate is yours.
You have given me everything my Lord,
but I have nothing to give you, in return.
In a state of complete gratitude and helplessness,
I drop this body of mine at your feet.

Most and more

• • •

Happiness is the way

When work is done as a choice, you tend to enjoy what you do, and when it is finally completed, you experience a sense of fulfilment. When work is undertaken as a compulsion, you struggle to do what you do, and when it is finally completed, you experience a sense of relief. Let us shift from the attitude of 'I must do it' to 'I WANT to do it'. If anyhow we have to do something, then might as well let us enjoy doing it. After all, there is no way to happiness. Happiness is the way.

Taj Mahal Moments

It is not enough that you create glorious moments, but also ensure that you celebrate those glorious moments. Always run your victory laps. Listen to the 'Aahaa' from your heart. It isn't the victory, but the joy of victory that's important. Let life wait... let the next experience wait... prolong the moments of celebration. Make your life a never-ending celebration.

Most of them couldn't control their tears. If spontaneous tears are believed to be the most honest of all human expressions, then the whole atmosphere was filled with unspoken honesty. Yes, they had been taught detached attachment and it seemed like they had understood it too. That's what they thought. But then to know that your eyes will never get to see *that* form again, your ears will never get to hear *that* voice again and most importantly, you will never get to experience *that* hug ever again, wasn't something people were ready to reconcile with. Does life care about your feelings?

Most and more

Will anything in the script of life change just because you are emotional? Whatever happens, happens and life moves on...

The faces also carried expressions of gratitude. In many ways, a part of them was actually him. Somewhere in the way they feel, the way they think, the way they act, why... even their body language had his influence. He always gave himself in total to them and in the process he became a part of them. Their mental scanners ran through the years they had been associated with him, the many special moments, many of which were life-changing. "I will never let you go," one of them said as he held his hand. "You can hold my hand, but you cannot hold on to me," Avyakta replied with a weak smile.

Lying on the cot was Avyakta, having chosen to enjoy the freedom of leaving his body in the midst of his loved ones, rather than in the confines of an ICU. Death is not an end, but the very crescendo of life, if one has lived purposefully. Death is the peaking of life, if one has lived dynamically. It was always his wish that he should be able to work up to the last day of his life. Till that Thursday, he had been active and he had reached out to people. Two days of tiredness and then as he woke up at sunrise on Sunday, he said, "I feel like sleeping. I think it is enough." He lay down on the cot and didn't get out of it. Food or water, anything that was offered to him, received the same response, "I think it is enough."

With a lot of hesitation and yet mustering the courage, something they had learnt from Avyakta - trust your spontaneity and speak your heart out, one of them asked, "What is the message of your life?" All heads turned towards the questioner. Some faces carried resistance, some displayed acceptance, but most were inquisitive, "What would Avyakta say?"

There was an elongated pause. Then there were a few attempted smiles, some deep breaths. Feeble, yet clear, the Voice said, "Actually, there are no secrets to my life. My life is an open book. I lived in the open. I lived amidst all of you. I was transparent. My life was there for everyone to see. There are actually no secrets."

There was so much silence, though Avyakta was actually talking. It seems a disciple once asked the Master, "What is the difference between you and us?" The Master replied, "Even when I am talking there is so much silence and even when you are silent, there is so much talking." It was exactly so. There was something very meditative about the moment.

A few more deep breaths and Avyakta continued, "All of you know that I've been very passionate about photography. Sometimes, years later, when you look at some pictures, you cannot actually recall where they were taken or who is in the picture. There are also pictures where you have fortunately written remarks on the rear, and on reading it your memory is refreshed and you are able to recall the location or the person. Of course, there are also some pictures, which allows you to relive the entire experience every time you look at them."

As the voice was a little feeble, people moved a little closer to the cot. One of them offered water and Avyakta repeated, "I think it is enough." He then added, "I can still vividly remember my first trip to Agra, though it was almost seven decades ago. As I entered the city of Agra, I was shocked by the filth, open drains, dry and dusty winds and the unpleasant odour in the air. I also went at a time when the weather made the city feel like a frying pan. That was a time when I hadn't yet discovered the art of being centred and happy, irrespective of the circumstances around me. Those days I needed a reason to be happy and Agra didn't provide me those reasons. I reluctantly kept following the guide and he let me walk past an entrance; suddenly, my breath stopped for a moment... there, in front of me, was the white magic... the marble marvel... humanity's pride and god's envy... the Taj Mahal. Even now as I am speaking to all of you, I can see the Taj Mahal. An impression was formed that death alone can erase. I don't need any photographs or write-ups in a journal to recall or relive my Taj Mahal moment. I just squatted before the Taj. For a few moments, I didn't know if I was even breathing. I didn't even blink. Aahaa!"

"You are asking me what is the message of my life?" Avyakta elaborated, "I not only created enough glorious moments in my life, but also took the time to enjoy these glorious moments. I took time out for the Taj Mahal moments of my life to sink into me. I allowed the feelings to seep into me before I marched onward and forward with life. I did not let my life be a parade of one experience after another, and then another, but I paused many times in life to feel the Taj Mahal moments of my life. For me, life was not just success, what next, again success and what next; it wasn't just a march past of moments... but after every glorious moment of my life, whether in the materialistic or the spiritual plane, I paused, I celebrated, I enjoyed the intoxication of life's experiences. I never needed liquor, for I drank so much of life and that was enough. I let it sink in till my heart said 'Aahaa', and only then moved on with life. So, one of the messages of my life is to create enough Taj Mahal moments in life and also take time to feel those Taj Mahal moments. I never lived life in a hurry.

Most and more

That doesn't mean I wasn't dynamic with life. In fact, I was more dynamic than most people I know. But I was certainly not into this neurotic restless running and running and running. Success is just empty success if you don't create moments of celebration around it."

Avyakta said, "You yearned for your dream car; now that the car has come, the stupid mind is already processing the next goal. You held the hand of the woman you always wanted, and now you don't have time for the honeymoon. You have finally moved into the house you laboured so much for, and now you don't have time to enjoy the house. The child you always wanted has finally come into this world, and you are at work for 14 hours. The curse of the present generation is that they no more have time to run their victory laps. Truly stupid!"

Avyakta's half-open and half-closed eyes looked into the eyes of all those present and he continued, "You train for four years for that moment. And then you realise the fruit of your four years of training happen in less than 10 seconds on the 100 metre Olympic track. There, you've crossed the finishing line first. The crowd in the entire stadium is on its feet. Millions of people all over the world are rejoicing this moment by watching you on their TV screens.

Now, run man, run, run your victory lap. Not just one, maybe two, why not three... run man, run your victory lap. This moment will not come again for four years. This is your moment. This is your Taj Mahal moment. Run your victory laps. Listen to the 'Aahaa' from your heart. It isn't the victory, but the joy of victory that we all have been waiting for... now that the moment has arrived, don't let it go by in a jiffy. Prolong the experience of your Taj Mahal moments. Let life wait... let the next experience wait... let the photographers wait, let the TV interview happen later... prolong this moment and enjoy this moment. Make your life a never-ending celebration."

With his eyes closed, he gently murmured, "I am not a person but a presence. With you always. Will be always. Wishing you most and more..." Then, after a long pause, they heard, "I think it is enough. I want to sleep." The Voice that always told them, "Very very gently open your eyes," for now closed his eyes. Avyakta, true to his name... was formless again.

One of them stepped forward, and feeling Avyakta's feet with her hands, she whispered with tears trickling down, "With you, with you. Without you too, with you. Feeling thy presence. Feeling thy grace. Feeling thy radiance. Will always be connected to you. Lead us through..."

Most and more

Somehow that day, though it was well beyond the normal time, the sun hadn't yet set. After all, where there is light, there cannot be darkness. Some candles keep burning even after the wax has completely melted.

You train for four years for that moment.
And then you realise the fruit of your four years of training happen in less than 10 seconds on the 100 metre Olympic track.
There, you've crossed the finishing line first.
The crowd in the entire stadium is on its feet.
Now, run man, run, run your victory lap.
Not just one, maybe two, why not three... run man, run your victory lap. This moment will not come again for four years. This is your moment.
Run your victory laps. Listen to the 'Aahaa' from your heart. It isn't the victory, but the joy of victory that we all have been waiting for... now that the moment has arrived, don't let it go by in a jiffy.
Let life wait... let the next experience wait... prolong this moment and enjoy this moment.
Make your life a never-ending celebration.

● ● ●

You were born to lead

Looking up to others is a positive trait, but it becomes a weakness when it leads you into submission. Look up without submitting yourself. You can become better than your boss. What is possible for one man is possible for all men. What one man can do, all men can do; in fact, do better. You were not born to follow. Remember, you were the leading sperm. Even as a sperm, you were not a follower. You were born to lead. Live up to your inheritance.

To know more about other life-changing instruments,
the Books, DVDs, Audio CDs, Audio Books, etc.,
please log on to
www.infinitheism.com